VOLUME 1

STAND
—— *on the* ——
WORD
Journal

A companion for your journey through the Bible

ADVANCING FAITH, FAMILY, AND FREEDOM

FIDELIS PUBLISHING ®

ISBN: 9781956454758

Stand on the Word Journal, Volume 1
© 2024 Tony Perkins

Content contributor: Dr. Kenyn Cureton
Interior layout design/typesetting: Lisa Parnell
Copyeditor: Lisa Parnell

Order at www.faithfultext.com for a significant discount. Email info@fidelis publishing.com to inquire about bulk purchase discounts.

Fidelis Publishing, LLC Winchester, VA•Nashville, TN www.fidelispublishing .com

Unless noted otherwise, Scripture quotations are taken from the Holy Bible, English Standard Version. ESV® Text Edition: 2016. Copyright © 2001 by Crossway Bibles, a publishing ministry of Good News Publishers.

Maps' geographic features courtesy of Bible Mapper (www.biblemapper.com).

Manufactured in the United States of America

10 9 8 7 6 5 4 3 2 1

FIDELIS
PUBLISHING

Contents

Introduction / 1

Daily Readings

Appendices

List of Maps and Diagrams

Contents

Welcome to the Stand on the Word Journal! Stand on the Word is a chronologically prioritized daily reading plan through the entire Bible. In other words, each reading takes you through the Bible as events occurred in history as far as it is possible. The plan is included in this daily journal. It can also be accessed at frc.org/Bible or simply by texting the word *Bible* to 67742, so invite your family and friends to join. As a companion on this daily journey through the Bible, we have created this journal to help you record your encounters with God along the way.

When I looked for a good devotional to use with my family, I came to the conclusion that nothing beats simply reading God's Word. Spend time reading and studying the Bible because it is literally "God-breathed" (2 Tim. 3:16). In other words, it is God's very words to us. The Bible answers the big questions like:

- Why am I here?
- Where did I come from?
- Where am I going (life after death)?
- If God is good, why does evil and suffering exist?

The Bible not only answers these big questions; it offers practical answers for questions such as:

- How can I deal with feelings of fear or anger or guilt?
- How can I forgive when I cannot forget?
- What should I look for in a spouse?
- How can I have a successful marriage?

- How can I be a good parent?
- What is my spiritual gift and place in the church?
- What is my stewardship responsibility as a citizen?

As a child, you may have learned the verse, "Your word is a lamp to my feet and a light to my path" (Psalm 119:105). God's Word shows the way forward in any area of life and on every question you face. Reading God's Word will help you establish a fruitful walk with the God who made you and loves you.

Whether you are single or married, the Stand on the Word Bible Reading Plan will enable you to lead your friends and family in daily reading of God's Word. The added benefit is you will all be reading the same text together. It will amaze you to see how God speaks sometimes in the same ways and at other times in different ways to each of you. Being on this journey together will build a spiritual synergy, deep bond, and sense of unity and purpose like nothing else you can do.

We provide you with a number of tools to help you on this journey. Foundational is the suggested daily reading from the Bible that only takes about ten to fifteen minutes to read. Also, join me most mornings for a brief Stand on the Word video devotional on the day's reading at www.frc.org/Bible. Additionally, we offer you a couple of reflection questions that you can use with your family or friends each day, maybe at breakfast or over the dinner table in the evening, or you can send each morning via text to your family or small group.

For example, at the same time each morning, whether I am at home, in Washington, or some foreign country, I send my wife and children a morning greeting along with a reminder of the passage for the day. The text includes two questions related to the daily reading. The questions are designed to help in content retention, serve as an accountability tool, and spark discussion. One of our favorite times as a family is Sunday when we gather to share what we heard from God in the Scriptures the previous week. It is amazing to watch the spiritual growth among our family members as we walk with God daily in His Word.

There are literally multiplied thousands of fellow believers who are following along with us on this journey, so welcome! We will pray for you as you Stand on the Word!

Standing (Eph. 6:13),
Tony Perkins

How to Use This Journal

The Stand on the Word Journal is designed to record your daily journey through God's Word and help you grab a screenshot of what He is saying and doing in your life. As you read God's Word chronologically, this journal will also help you keep track of where you are in the greater story of Scripture. We provide you with several helpful tools at the back of this resource to enrich your experience with God in His Word.

Here are a few suggestions for getting the most from your time in God's Word and your Stand on the Word Journal:

1. Try to read your Bible at a set time and place every day until it becomes a habit. Early in the morning before your day starts is best. Set a reminder or make an appointment on your phone. If you miss a day or two, don't quit. Make it up and keep going.

2. As you begin each week, read the brief introductory question meant to help you anticipate what you will be reading that week.

3. When you start a new book of the Bible, you will be directed to the appendix for the introduction to that book. We provide a brief overview of what you will be reading as to the author, date, purpose in writing, a general outline, main messages, and how the book anticipates or reflects on Jesus.

4. We suggest you navigate each day's entry by first reading the "Verse of the Day," then dive into the full passage in "Today's Reading." Once you finish, engage the two reflection and discussion questions. Then write down what God may be saying to you, your thoughts and insights from the reading, and maybe a prayer to God of repentance or gratitude or praise or even a resolve to make a change. Your journal truly is a blank canvas for you to capture your walk with God in His Word.

5. Invite others to join you on this journey. Encourage your family or a group of friends to follow along. Even if they don't have this journal, they can join you at www.frc.org/Bible. In addition to the daily questions, small-group discussion questions are provided for Sunday. You will be amazed at the spiritual synergy that occurs as you take this journey together.

How to Get the Most Out of Bible Study

Here are five habits to cultivate as you approach God's Word each day.

1. **Read it through:** Don't skip around. Read the entire selection of Scripture. If you are pressed for time, please read the Bible before you read the study guide notes. So read it through.

2. **Think it over:** Meditate on it. Let it marinate in your mind. If you can, take notes. We provide a notes page at the end of each day. Think it over.

3. **Pray it in:** Personalize the Scripture. Turn the verse that speaks to you into a prayer, and then pray it into your life. Ask God what you need to do in response. That leads us to the next habit.

4. **Live it out:** Consider ways to apply what God is revealing to you, ways you can obey Him.

Put His Word into practice. Make it a part of who you are, how you think, how you speak, and behave toward God and other people. In other words, take God's Word and live it out.

5. **Pass it on.** Don't keep it to yourself. People are in your life who need the same truth God has spoken to you in His Word. Share it. Pass it on.

About Stand on the Word

Stand on the Word is a ministry of Family Research Council, whose mission is to serve in the kingdom of God by championing faith, family, and freedom in public policy and the culture from a biblical worldview. The purpose of Stand on the Word is to lay the foundation for a biblical worldview through daily reading and application of God's Word.

Week 1

Where did we come from, what went wrong with the world, and is there any hope? Find out this week as we begin Genesis.

For an introduction to Genesis, see appendix 1, page 383.

— DAY 1 —

Today's Reading: Genesis 1–3

Verse of the Day:

These are the generations
of the heavens and the earth when they were created,
in the day that the LORD God made the earth and the
heavens. — Genesis 2:4

Questions for Reflection and Discussion

1. What do you think it means that humankind was created in the "image" of God (see 1:26–28)?

2. What was the serpent (Satan) doing by asking Eve, "Did God actually say, 'You shall not eat of any tree in the garden'?" (3:1)?

Notes on Today's Bible Reading

_____

_____

_____

_____

_____

_____

_____

_____

— DAY 2 —
Today's Reading: Genesis 4–5

Verse of the Day:

"If you do well, will you not be accepted? And if you do not do well, sin is crouching at the door. Its desire is contrary to you, but you must rule over it." — Genesis 4:7

Questions for Reflection and Discussion

1. What do you think God was communicating to Cain when He said, "[S]in is crouching at the door. Its desire is contrary to you, but you must rule over it" (4:7b)?

2. Who "walked with God, and he was not, for God took him" (5:21–24)?
   a. Seth
   b. Enoch
   c. Methuselah
   d. None of the above

Notes on Today's Bible Reading

— DAY 3 —
Today's Reading: Genesis 6–9

Verse of the Day:

The Lord saw that the wickedness of man was great in the earth, and that every intention of the thoughts of his heart was only evil continually. — Genesis 6:5

Questions for Reflection and Discussion

1. What was the condition of the earth when God declared to Noah that He would destroy it (6:5, 13)?

2. What was the sign of the covenant God gave Noah that He would never again destroy the earth by flood?
   a. A comet in the sky
   b. His rainbow in the cloud
   c. A fire on the mountain
   d. A sunset on the sea

Notes on Today's Bible Reading

— DAY 4 —
Today's Reading: Genesis 10–13

Verse of the Day:

Then they said, "Come, let us build ourselves a city and a tower with its top in the heavens, and let us make a name for ourselves, lest we be dispersed over the face of the whole earth." — Genesis 11:4

Questions for Reflection and Discussion

1. While God did not approve of the motivation behind the building of the tower of Babel, what did He point to as a key to their achievement (11:6)?
    a. They had superior building materials.
    b. They had a smart design.
    c. They had clever engineering.
    d. They were unified.

2. What did God commit to do for those who blessed Abram as God led him out to begin a new nation (12:1–3)?

Notes on Today's Bible Reading

_____

_____

_____

_____

_____

_____

_____

_____

_____

_____

Journey of Abram to the Promised Land

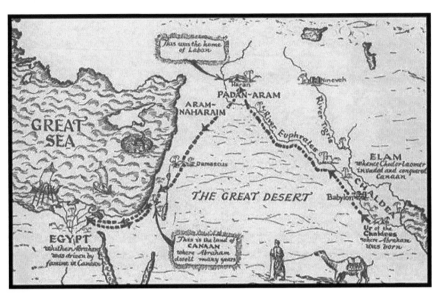

https://www.blueletterbible.org/images/ TheGraphicBible/imageDisplay/tgb_019_b

— DAY 5 —

Today's Reading: Genesis 14–17

Verse of the Day:

After these things the word of the LORD came to Abram in a vision: "Fear not, Abram, I am your shield; your reward shall be very great." — Genesis 15:1

Questions for Reflection and Discussion

1. In these chapters, what was the first of many problems for Lot when he lived in Sodom (14:8–12)?
   a. He got in a bidding war for a house.
   b. He got into trouble with the HOA.
   c. He became a POW and had to be rescued.
   d. None of the above.

2. What did God reveal to Abram about his descendants (chap. 15)?

Notes on Today's Bible Reading

— DAY 6 —

Today's Reading: Genesis 18–19

Verse of the Day:

"For I have chosen him, that he may command his children and his household after him to keep the way of the LORD by doing righteousness and justice, so that the LORD may bring to Abraham what he has promised him." — Genesis 18:19

Questions for Reflection and Discussion

1. How did Abraham respond to the message that God was going to destroy Sodom and Gomorrah because of the people's sin (18:22–33)?
    a. He celebrated their impending judgment.
    b. He objected that the punishment was too harsh.
    c. He interceded repeatedly.
    d. None of the above.

2. What did the men of Sodom do when Lot appealed to them not to sexually assault the strangers who were staying in Lot's house (19:4–9)?

Notes on Today's Bible Reading

— DAY 7 —
Review of This Week's Readings:
Genesis 1–19

Questions for Reflection and Discussion

1. What passage uniquely spoke to you this week?
2. What insights did you gain about God?
3. What application might this have to what is happening in the world today?
4. How would God have you apply this truth to your life?

Notes from Reflecting on This Week's Bible Readings

How can God use imperfect people in imperfect families to accomplish His purposes? Find out as we continue our journey through Genesis.

— DAY 1 —
Today's Reading: Genesis 20–22

Verse of the Day:

So Abraham called the name of that place, "The LORD will provide"; as it is said to this day, "On the mount of the LORD it shall be provided." — Genesis 22:14

Questions for Reflection and Discussion

1. Why did Abraham tell Abimelech that Sarah was his sister and not his wife?
   a. He believed there was no fear of God there.
   b. He believed he would be killed because of her.
   c. Both of the above.
   d. Neither of the above.

2. How did God test Abraham regarding his son Isaac (chap. 22)?

Notes on Today's Bible Reading

_____

_____

_____

_____

_____

_____

_____

_____

— DAY 2 —

Today's Reading: Genesis 23–24

Verse of the Day:

"The LORD, the God of heaven, who took me from my father's house and from the land of my kindred, and who spoke to me and swore to me, 'To your offspring I will give this land,' he will send his angel before you, and you shall take a wife for my son from there." — Genesis 24:7

Questions for Reflection and Discussion

1. By the end of chapter 23, what property did Abraham own in the promised land?
2. Where did Abraham's servant (Eliezer) turn for help in finding a wife for Isaac (24:12)?
   a. A matchmaker
   b. A dating app
   c. Yahweh, God of Abraham
   d. None of the above

Notes on Today's Bible Reading

— DAY 3 —

Today's Reading: Genesis 25–26

Verse of the Day:

And Isaac sowed in that land and reaped in the same year a hundred-fold. The LORD blessed him. — Genesis 26:12

Questions for Reflection and Discussion

1. What did Isaac and Ishmael come together to do (25:7–9)?

2. What did Isaac do that was just like his father (26:1–11)?
   a. Sought refuge with the Philistines during a famine
   b. Lied about his wife
   c. Was confronted for his deception by a pagan king
   d. All of the above

Notes on Today's Bible Reading

— DAY 4 —

Today's Reading: Genesis 27–28

Verse of the Day:

"Behold, I am with you and will keep you wherever you go, and will bring you back to this land. For I will not leave you until I have done what I have promised you." — Genesis 28:15

Questions for Reflection and Discussion

1. What, unfortunately, family behavior do we see in this passage?
2. What did this deception do to the family?

Notes on Today's Bible Reading

— DAY 5 —

Today's Reading: Genesis 29–30

Verse of the Day:

But Laban said to him, "If I have found favor in your sight, I have learned by divination that the LORD has blessed me because of you." — Genesis 30:27

Questions for Reflection and Discussion

1. What is the stated reason God opened the womb of Leah?

2. What was one of the main reasons Laban said he wanted Jacob to stay and continue serving him?

Notes on Today's Bible Reading

— DAY 6 —

Today's Reading: Genesis 31–33

Verse of the Day:

Then [the Lord] said, "Let me go, for the day has broken." But Jacob said, "I will not let you go unless you bless me." — Genesis 32:26

Questions for Reflection and Discussion

1. Laban took advantage of Jacob, even changing his wages ten times. What do Laban's efforts and the outcome tell us about God's involvement with our employment?

2. As Jacob wrestled with God, he did not let Him go until God did what?
   a. Declared him the winner
   b. Blessed him
   c. Dislocated his hip
   d. None of the above

Notes on Today's Bible Reading

— DAY 7 —
Review of This Week's Readings:
Genesis 20–33

Questions for Reflection and Discussion

1. What passage uniquely spoke to you this week?

2. What insights did you gain about God?

3. What application might this have to what is happening in the world today?

4. How would God have you apply this truth to your life?

Notes from Reflecting on This Week's Bible Readings

How can God turn what is meant for evil into good? Find out as we read about Joseph.

— DAY 1 —

Today's Reading: Genesis 34–36

Verse of the Day:

And God said to him, "Your name is Jacob; no longer shall your name be called Jacob, but Israel shall be your name." So he called his name Israel. — Genesis 35:10

Questions for Reflection and Discussion

1. What was Jacob's response to the actions of Simeon and Levi?

2. What actions might Jacob have taken that would have averted the massacre at Shechem?

Notes on Today's Bible Reading

_____

_____

_____

_____

_____

_____

_____

_____

_____

_____

_____

— DAY 2 —
Today's Reading: Genesis 37–39

Verse of the Day:

But the LORD was with Joseph and showed him steadfast love and gave him favor in the sight of the keeper of the prison. — Genesis 39:21

Questions for Reflection and Discussion

1. What made the difference between the lives of Er and Joseph?
2. What were the two trespasses Judah committed?

Notes on Today's Bible Reading

— DAY 3 —

Today's Reading: Genesis 40–41

Verses of the Day:

Then Pharaoh said to Joseph, "Since God has shown you all
this, there is none so discerning and wise as you are. You shall
be over my house, and all my people shall order themselves as
you command. Only as regards the throne will I be greater than
you." — Genesis 41:39–40

Questions for Reflection and Discussion

1. Why did Pharaoh select Joseph to oversee the collection and distribution of grain?

2. What is the reason given for the repeating of Pharaoh's dream?

Notes on Today's Bible Reading

— DAY 4 —

Today's Reading: Genesis 42–44

Verse of the Day:

Then they said, . . . "In truth we are guilty concerning our brother, in that we saw the distress of his soul, when he begged us and we did not listen. That is why this distress has come upon us." — Genesis 42:21

Questions for Reflection and Discussion

1. When Joseph's brothers encountered trouble in Egypt, what did they attribute it to?

2. What does this tell us about unconfessed sin?

Notes on Today's Bible Reading

— DAY 5 —

Today's Reading: Genesis 45–47

Verse of the Day:

"And now do not be distressed or angry with yourselves because you sold me here, for God sent me before you to preserve life." — Genesis 45:5

Questions for Reflection and Discussion

1. What evidence do we see that shows Joseph did not harbor unforgiveness toward his brothers? Who did Joseph say caused him to be sent to Egypt?

2. Listening to God, Jacob took his entire family (children and grandchildren) to Egypt during the famine. While the Egyptians were selling their livestock and land for grain to eat, what happened to Jacob and his family?

Notes on Today's Bible Reading

_____

_____

_____

_____

_____

_____

_____

_____

_____

_____

_____

_____

— DAY 6 —
Today's Reading: Genesis 48–50

Verse of the Day:

"As for you, you meant evil against me, but God meant it for good, to bring it about that many people should be kept alive, as they are today." — Genesis 50:20

Questions for Reflection and Discussion

1. What did Joseph tell his brother when their father, Jacob, died?
2. How old was Joseph when he died?

Notes on Today's Bible Reading

— DAY 7 —
Review of This Week's Readings:
Genesis 34–50

Questions for Reflection and Discussion

1. What passage uniquely spoke to you this week?

2. What insights did you gain about God?

3. What application might this have to what is happening in the world today?

4. How would God have you apply this truth to your life?

Notes from Reflecting on This Week's Bible Readings

Week 4

What assurance do believers have through suffering? Find out this week in Job.

For an introduction to Job, see appendix 1, page 383.

— DAY 1 —

Today's Reading: Job 1–4

Verse of the Day:

And the LORD said to Satan, "Have you considered my servant Job, that there is none like him on the earth, a blameless and upright man, who fears God and turns away from evil?" — Job 1:8

Questions for Reflection and Discussion

1. How did Job come to the attention of Satan?
2. God set limits on what Satan can do. What does this tell us about Satan's power?

Notes on Today's Bible Reading

— DAY 2 —

Today's Reading: Job 5–8

Verse of the Day:

"Behold, blessed is the one whom God reproves; therefore despise not the discipline of the Almighty." — Job 5:17

Questions for Reflection and Discussion

1. How did Job's friend Eliphaz interpret Job's grievous situation?
2. Where did Job believe his affliction was coming from?

Notes on Today's Bible Reading

— DAY 3 —

Today's Reading: Job 9–12

Verses of the Day:

"For he is not a man, as I am, that I might answer him,
    that we should come to trial together.
There is no arbiter between us,
    who might lay his hand on us both. — Job 9:32–33

Questions for Reflection and Discussion

1. Job lamented that God was not like a man—where he could talk to God or go to court to resolve their differences. He also pointed to something he did not have, which we do in the New Testament. What was it?
    a. Courts
    b. Mediator
    c. Doctor
    d. None of the above

2. What did Zophar tell Job he should do?

Notes on Today's Bible Reading

_____

_____

_____

_____

_____

_____

_____

_____

_____

_____

_____

— DAY 4 —
Today's Reading: Job 13–16

Verses of the Day:

"I also could speak as you do,
> if you were in my place;
I could join words together against you
> And shake my head at you.
I could strengthen you with my mouth,
> and the solace of my lips would assuage your pain." — Job 16:4–5

Questions for Reflection and Discussion

1. Job talked about how a tree is better off than a man because it can sprout again. We know the end of Job's story, but he didn't during his trial; as a result, he was discouraged and ready to die. What can we learn about difficulty from the life of Job?

2. Job said, "Though he [God] slay me, I will _____ ___ _____."

Notes on Today's Bible Reading

_____

_____

_____

_____

_____

_____

_____

_____

_____

_____

— DAY 5 —

Today's Reading: Job 17–20

Verse of the Day:

"For I know that my Redeemer lives, and at the last he will stand upon the earth." — Job 19:25

Questions for Reflection and Discussion

1. Job's friends ratcheted up their rhetoric, which sent Job into even more profound despair. In Job's response, we get a glimpse of the total rejection and misery he was enduring. What was the one thing he held onto that gave him hope?

2. What can we learn from how Job's friends responded to his situation?

Notes on Today's Bible Reading

— DAY 6 —

Today's Reading: Job 21–24

Verses of the Day:

"My foot has held fast to his steps;
> I have kept his way and have not turned aside.
I have not departed from the commandment of his lips;
> I have treasured the words of his mouth more than my portion of
> food." — Job 23:11–12

Questions for Reflection and Discussion

1. Although everyone told Job he is to blame for his troubles, he was confident that is not the case even though he was suffering and couldn't explain the reasons. What gave Job this confidence?

2. What point was Job making in the second portion of his response to Eliphaz?

Notes on Today's Bible Reading

— DAY 7 —
Review of This Week's Readings:
Job 1–24

Questions for Reflection and Discussion

1. What passage uniquely spoke to you this week?

2. What insights did you gain about God?

3. What application might this have to what is happening in the world today?

4. How would God have you apply this truth to your life?

Notes from Reflecting on This Week's Bible Readings

Week 5

How does God respond to complaints about our circumstances? Find out as we conclude studying the book of Job.

— DAY 1 —

Today's Reading: Job 25–29

Verse of the Day:

And he said to man,
"Behold, the fear of the LORD, that is wisdom,
  and to turn away from evil is understanding." — Job 28:28

Questions for Reflection and Discussion

1. What do you think Job was communicating about God in his response to Bildad in 26:14?

2. What do you think enabled Job to say, "[M]y heart does not reproach me for any of my days"?

Notes on Today's Bible Reading

— DAY 2 —
Today's Reading: Job 30–32

Verse of the Day:

"Did not I weep for him whose day was hard? Was not my soul grieved for the needy?" — Job 30:25

Questions for Reflection and Discussion

1. How did Job's standing in the community change as a result of his tribulation?

2. Job made a covenant with his eyes to do what?

Notes on Today's Bible Reading

— DAY 3 —
Today's Reading: Job 33–35

Verse of the Day:

"The Spirit of God has made me, and the breath of the Almighty gives me life." — Job 33:4

Questions for Reflection and Discussion

1. Elihu, the youngest of Job's "friends," was now compelled to speak. There is wisdom in some of his words, but what is missing in his comments is something the apostle Paul wrote about in Romans 11:33.

2. What did Job's friends fail to recognize or acknowledge in Job's situation?

Notes on Today's Bible Reading

— DAY 4 —
Today's Reading: Job 36–38

Verse of the Day:

"Hear this, O Job;
      stop and consider the wondrous works of God." — Job 37:14

Questions for Reflection and Discussion

1. What did Elihu point to in this passage as evidence of God's greatness and power of God?

2. How did Elihu refute his own determination that Job's sufferings were the result of disobedience or rebellion? (Hint: 36:26)

Notes on Today's Bible Reading

— DAY 5 —

Today's Reading: Job 39–40

Verses of the Day:

"Behold, I am of small account; what shall I answer you?
I lay my hand on my mouth. . . . I will proceed no further." — Job 40:4–5

Questions for Reflection and Discussion

1. How did Job respond to God?
2. Why do you think Job responded in this way?

Notes on Today's Bible Reading

— DAY 6 —

Today's Reading: Job 41–42

Verse of the Day:

And the LORD restored the fortunes of Job, when he had prayed for his friends. And the LORD gave Job twice as much as he had before. — Job 42:10

Questions for Reflection and Discussion

1. What point was God making to Job as He described the power of both the behemoth and leviathan?

2. God restored all that Job had lost when Job did what?

Notes on Today's Bible Reading

— DAY 7 —
Review of This Week's Readings:
Job 25–42

Questions for Reflection and Discussion

1. What passage uniquely spoke to you this week?

2. What insights did you gain about God?

3. What application might this have to what is happening in the world today?

4. How would God have you apply this truth to your life?

Notes from Reflecting on This Week's Bible Readings

Week 6

How does God deliver His people from bondage? Find out this week in Exodus.

For an introduction to Exodus, see appendix 1, page 384.

— DAY 1 —

Today's Reading: Exodus 1–3

Verse of the Day:

But the midwives feared God and did not do as the king of Egypt commanded them, but let the male children live. — Exodus 1:17

Questions for Reflection and Discussion

1. Why did the midwives not obey the king's order to kill the newborn boys?
2. What was God's response to the midwives?

Notes on Today's Bible Reading

— DAY 2 —

Today's Reading: Exodus 4–6

Verse of the Day:

"Go in, tell Pharaoh king of Egypt to let the people of Israel go out of his land." — Exodus 6:11

Questions for Reflection and Discussion

1. What excuse did Moses use to say he could not do as God asked?

2. From this passage, what do we see can happen when we step out in obedience to God? And what is that response designed to do?

Notes on Today's Bible Reading

— DAY 3 —

Today's Reading: Exodus 7–8

Verse of the Day:

"You shall speak all that I command you, and your brother
Aaron shall tell Pharaoh to let the people of Israel go out of his
land." — Exodus 7:2

Questions for Reflection and Discussion

1. Why do you think the Lord waited until the fourth plague to distinguish between the Egyptians and the Israelites?

2. A powerful testimony of a yielded servant is found in 8:13. Here was a man who had a hard time speaking (Exod. 4:10), and God was doing what?

Notes on Today's Bible Reading

— DAY 4 —

Today's Reading: Exodus 9–10

Verses of the Day:

"[T]hat I may show these signs of mine among them, and that you may tell in the hearing of your son and of your grandson how I have dealt harshly with the Egyptians and what signs I have done . . . that you may know that I am the LORD." — Exodus 10:1–2

Questions for Reflection and Discussion

1. What was the difference in how Pharaoh's heart was hardened after the fifth and sixth plagues?

2. Was Moses willing to negotiate with Pharaoh concerning what God instructed him to ask Pharaoh to let them do?

Notes on Today's Bible Reading

— DAY 5 —
Today's Reading: Exodus 11–12

Verse of the Day:

"But not a dog shall growl against any of the people of Israel, either man or beast, that you may know that the LORD makes a distinction between Egypt and Israel." — Exodus 11:7

Questions for Reflection and Discussion

1. As they left Egypt, how were the children of Israel partially compensated for their forced labor?

2. Name one of the several parallels between the Passover lamb and Jesus.

Notes on Today's Bible Reading

— DAY 6 —

Today's Reading: Exodus 13–14

Verses of the Day:

And Moses said to the people, "Fear not, stand firm, and see the salvation of the LORD, . . . The LORD will fight for you, and you have only to be silent." — Exodus 14:13–14

Questions for Reflection and Discussion

1. What was the purpose of the seven days of unleavened bread (Passover feast) for future generations?

2. The children of Israel went out of Egypt with boldness, but it wasn't long until the Egyptians were chasing them, and their courage was replaced with fear. How did Moses respond to the Israelites?

Notes on Today's Bible Reading

— DAY 7 —
Review of This Week's Readings:
Exodus 1–14

Questions for Reflection and Discussion

1. What passage uniquely spoke to you this week?

2. What insights did you gain about God?

3. What application might this have to what is happening in the world today?

4. How would God have you apply this truth to your life?

Notes from Reflecting on This Week's Bible Readings

What is on God's top-ten list for us?
Find out as we continue reading
in Exodus.

— DAY 1 —
Today's Reading: Exodus 15–16

Verse of the Day:

"Who is like you, O LORD, among the gods?
Who is like you, majestic in holiness,
awesome in glorious deeds, doing wonders? — Exodus 15:11

Questions for Reflection and Discussion

1. In the song composed by Moses upon the destruction of the pursuing Egyptian army, Moses said the Egyptians were destroyed for what reason?

2. What was the first conditional promise God made to the children of Israel after they left Egypt?

Notes on Today's Bible Reading

— DAY 2 —

Today's Reading: Exodus 17–19

Verse of the Day:

"[L]ook for able men from all the people, men who fear God, who are trustworthy and hate a bribe, and place such men over the people as chiefs of thousands, of hundreds, of fifties, and of tens." — Exodus 18:21

Questions for Reflection and Discussion

1. How did the children of Israel "tempt" the Lord when they were camped in Rephidim?

2. In the advice Jethro gave Moses regarding organizing this new nation, he told Moses to do what with the people?

Notes on Today's Bible Reading

— DAY 3 —

Today's Reading: Exodus 20–22

Verse of the Day:

"In every place where I cause my name to be remembered I will come to you and bless you." — Exodus 20:24b

Questions for Reflection and Discussion

1. These passages record the elements of the Mosaic covenant, which is identified by the _____ Commandments.

2. Which commandment is associated with a warning of its impact upon subsequent generations?

Notes on Today's Bible Reading

— DAY 4 —

Today's Reading: Exodus 23–25

Verse of the Day:

"[Y]ou shall not bow down to their gods nor serve them, nor do as they do, but you shall utterly overthrow them and break their pillars in pieces." — Exodus 23:24

Questions for Reflection and Discussion

1. To confuse the inhabitants of Canaan, what did God promise to send before the children of Israel?

2. God told Moses to collect an offering of the materials needed to build the tabernacle. What was to be the attitude of those who gave?

Notes on Today's Bible Reading

The Tabernacle

Washbasin   Meeting Tent   Lampstand   Incense Altar   Most Holy Place

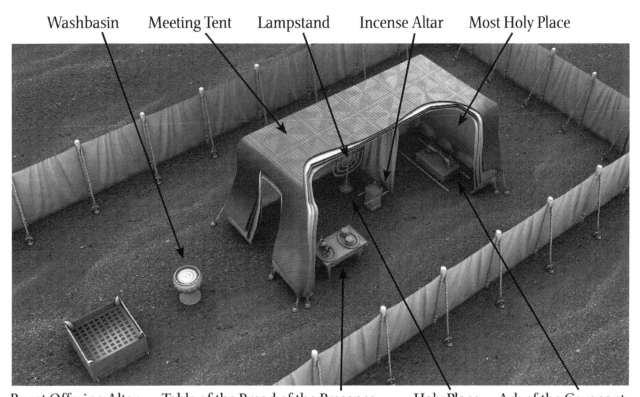

Burnt Offering Altar   Table of the Bread of the Presence   Holy Place   Ark of the Covenant

Image courtesy of The Readable Bible (www.readablebible.com)

— DAY 5 —

Today's Reading: Exodus 26–27

Verse of the Day:

"And you shall hang the veil . . . and bring the ark of the testimony in there within the veil. And the veil shall separate for you the Holy Place from the Most Holy." — Exodus 26:33

Questions for Reflection and Discussion

1. What, if anything, can we understand about worshipping God based upon His instructions regarding the tabernacle?

2. What was behind the veil in the tabernacle?

Notes on Today's Bible Reading

— DAY 6 —

Today's Reading: Exodus 28

Verse of the Day:

"You shall make a plate of pure gold and engrave on it, like the engraving of a signet, 'Holy to the Lord.'" — Exodus 28:36

Questions for Reflection and Discussion

1. Who was Moses instructed to select to make the garments for the priests?

2. What does this passage say about where vocational skills come from and how we are to use them?

Notes on Today's Bible Reading

— DAY 7 —
Review of This Week's Readings:
Exodus 15–28

Questions for Reflection and Discussion

1. What passage uniquely spoke to you this week?

2. What insights did you gain about God?

3. What application might this have to what is happening in the world today?

4. How would God have you apply this truth to your life?

Notes from Reflecting on This Week's Bible Readings

What does the tabernacle teach us about God? Find out as we finish Exodus this week.

— DAY 1 —
Today's Reading: Exodus 29

Verses of the Day:

"I will dwell among the people of Israel and will be their God. And they shall know that I am the LORD their God, who brought them out of the land of Egypt that I might dwell among them. I am the LORD their God." — Exodus 29:45–46

Questions for Reflection and Discussion

1. What does it mean to consecrate or sanctify?

2. Why do you think it was important that the priests be consecrated for service in the tabernacle?

Notes on Today's Bible Reading

— DAY 2 —

Today's Reading: Exodus 30–32

Verse of the Day:

"And I have given to all able men ability, that they may make all that I have commanded you." — Exodus 31:6b

Questions for Reflection and Discussion

1. Who ultimately appointed the artisans who designed and built the tabernacle?

2. What example did God provide as it pertained to the Sabbath?

Notes on Today's Bible Reading

_____

_____

_____

_____

_____

_____

_____

_____

_____

_____

_____

_____

_____

_____

_____

_____

— DAY 3 —

Today's Reading: Exodus 33–34

Verse of the Day:

"For I will cast out nations before you and enlarge your borders; no one shall covet your land, when you go up to appear before the LORD your God three times in the year." — Exodus 34:24

Questions for Reflection and Discussion

1. Moses did not want to go into the promised land without what going with them?

2. Why do you think the Lord warned the children of Israel not to make covenants/treaties with the inhabitants of the land into which they were going?

Notes on Today's Bible Reading

— DAY 4 —

Today's Reading: Exodus 35–36

Verse of the Day:

And they came, everyone whose heart stirred him, and everyone whose spirit moved him, and brought the LORD's contribution to be used for the tent of meeting, and for all its service, and for the holy garments. — Exodus 35:21

Questions for Reflection and Discussion

1. Where did most of the gold, silver, and bronze come from, which the people gave to construct the tabernacle and garments for the priests?

2. What did the craftsmen, who were working on the sanctuary, tell Moses about the offering of the people? It was:
   a. Too skimpy
   b. Just right
   c. Too much
   d. None of the above

Notes on Today's Bible Reading

— DAY 5 —

Today's Reading: Exodus 37–38

Verse of the Day:

These are the records of the tabernacle, the tabernacle of the testimony, as they were recorded at the commandment of Moses, the responsibility of the Levites under the direction of Ithamar the son of Aaron the priest. — Exodus 38:21

Questions for Reflection and Discussion

1. Do you think there was a reason God provided explicit instruction on the design of the tabernacle rather than allowing Moses to design it?

2. What was the age at which the men were included in the census? Why do you think that age was chosen?

Notes on Today's Bible Reading

— DAY 6 —
Today's Reading: Exodus 39–40

Verse of the Day:

For the cloud of the LORD was on the tabernacle by day, and fire was in it by night, in the sight of all the house of Israel throughout all their journeys. — Exodus 40:38

Questions for Reflection and Discussion

1. What did Moses do when the artisans and craftsmen completed their work?

2. When the tabernacle was set up, what happened when the cloud covered it?

Notes on Today's Bible Reading

— DAY 7 —
Review of This Week's Readings:
Exodus 29–40

Questions for Reflection and Discussion

1. What passage uniquely spoke to you this week?

2. What insights did you gain about God?

3. What application might this have to what is happening in the world today?

4. How would God have you apply this truth to your life?

Notes from Reflecting on This Week's Bible Readings

Week 9

What is the message behind God's specific requirements for Israel? Find out as we begin reading Leviticus.

For an introduction to Leviticus, see appendix 1, page 385.

— DAY 1 —

Today's Reading: Leviticus 1–3

Verses of the Day:

The LORD called Moses and spoke to him from the tent of meeting, saying, "Speak to the people of Israel and say to them, When any one of you brings an offering to the LORD, you shall bring your offering of livestock from the herd or from the flock." — Leviticus 1:1–2

Questions for Reflection and Discussion

1. Why do you think God was so explicit in what and how offerings were to be made?

2. What are we to offer to God under the new covenant? (Hint: Rom. 12:1–2)

Notes on Today's Bible Reading

_____

_____

_____

_____

_____

_____

_____

_____

_____

_____

— DAY 2 —

Today's Reading: Leviticus 4–6

Verse of the Day:

"And the priest shall make atonement for him for the sin which he has committed, and he shall be forgiven." — Leviticus 4:35b

Questions for Reflection and Discussion

1. What type of offering was a person to bring if they unintentionally or unknowingly sinned?

2. According to this passage, lying to one's neighbor about that neighbor's property is a sin against whom?

Notes on Today's Bible Reading

— DAY 3 —
Today's Reading: Leviticus 7–9

Verses of the Day:

"[T]he glory of the Lord appeared to all the people. And fire came out from before the Lord and consumed the burnt offering . . . , and when all the people saw it, they shouted and fell on their faces." — Leviticus 9:23b–24

Questions for Reflection and Discussion

1. What was the purpose of the peace offering?
2. In this passage, how was the anointing oil used?

Notes on Today's Bible Reading

— DAY 4 —
Today's Reading: Leviticus 10–12

Verse of the Day:

Then Moses said to Aaron, "This is what the LORD has said: 'Among those who are near me I will be sanctified, and before all the people I will be glorified.'" And Aaron held his peace." — Leviticus 10:3

Questions for Reflection and Discussion

1. Why were Nadab and Abihu consumed by fire from the Lord?

2. Through Moses what was the Lord's message about how people are to approach Him?

Notes on Today's Bible Reading

— DAY 5 —

Today's Reading: Leviticus 13–14

Verse of the Day:

"The leprous person who has the disease shall wear torn clothes and let the hair of his head hang loose, and he shall cover his upper lip and cry out, 'Unclean, unclean.'" — Leviticus 13:45

Questions for Reflection and Discussion

1. When a person had what appeared to be leprosy, they were declared "unclean" and isolated for some time. This isolation had both spiritual and physical implications. Why was the person isolated or quarantined?

2. Based upon isolation over the physical concerns, do we see anything similar to this today?

Notes on Today's Bible Reading

— DAY 6 —

Today's Reading: Leviticus 15–16

Verse of the Day:

"For on this day shall atonement be made for you to cleanse you. You shall be clean before the LORD from all your sins." — Leviticus 16:30

Questions for Reflection and Discussion

1. The reasons for the cleansing guidelines were:
   a. Spiritual/ritual
   b. Physical/health
   c. Neither
   d. Both *a.* and *b.*

2. What is a scapegoat?

Notes on Today's Bible Reading

— DAY 7 —
Review of This Week's Readings:
Leviticus 1–16

Questions for Reflection and Discussion

1. What passage uniquely spoke to you this week?

2. What insights did you gain about God?

3. What application might this have to what is happening in the world today?

4. How would God have you apply this truth to your life?

Notes from Reflecting on This Week's Bible Readings

_____

_____

_____

_____

_____

_____

_____

_____

_____

_____

_____

_____

_____

_____

_____

Week 10

How should God's people live in a corrupt culture? Find out as we conclude studying in the book of Leviticus.

— DAY 1 —

Today's Reading: Leviticus 17–18

Verse of the Day:

"[K]eep my statutes and my rules; if a person does them, he shall live by them: I am the Lord." — Leviticus 18:5

Questions for Reflection and Discussion

1. Instruction is given not to consume blood, and the reasons are life is in the blood and blood is shed for a purpose. What is that purpose?

2. The children of Israel were instructed to not conduct themselves in the same way as those who occupied the land of Canaan. Is there a biblical principle in the instruction that applies to us? If so, what is it?

Notes on Today's Bible Reading

_____

_____

_____

_____

_____

_____

_____

_____

— DAY 2 —

Today's Reading: Leviticus 19–21

Verses of the Day:

"Consecrate yourselves, therefore, and be holy, for I am the Lord your God. Keep my statutes and do them; I am the Lord who sanctifies you." — Leviticus 20:7–8

Questions for Reflection and Discussion

1. What personal provisions for caring for the poor are outlined in this passage?

2. What is the equivalent of this practice/principle today?

Notes on Today's Bible Reading

The Festivals of the Lord[a]

A sacred convocation is held on the first day of each festival. The offerings are in addition to the regular daily offerings, Sabbath offerings, and new moon offerings (see Numbers 28:3–15).

English Name	Spring Festivals				Fall Festivals		
	Passover[c]	**Unleavened Bread**[c]	**Firstfruits**	**Weeks**[c] (Pentecost, Harvest)	**Trumpets**	**Day of Atonement**	**Shelters**[c] (a.k.a. Tabernacles, Booths, Ingathering)
Hebrew Name	Pesach	Hag Hamatzot	Bikkurim	Shavuot	Rosh Hashanah	Yom Kippur	Sukkot
Purpose	Remember God passed over the Israelites when, to free them, he killed the firstborn of Egypt.	Remember leaving Egypt.	Recognize God's goodness in providing a crop.	Celebrate the grain harvest and God's giving of the Ten Commandments.	Celebrate the beginning of the new year.	Mourn sin, afflict the soul, and seek atonement.	Remember the exodus and forty years of wandering.
Dates[b] **Hebrew**	Abib 14	Abib 15–21	Abib 16	50th day after Passover	Tishri 1	Tishri 10	Tishri 15
Gregorian	Late March to late April			Mid-May to mid-June		Mid-September to mid-October	
Number of Days	One day	Six or seven days	One day	One day	One day	One day	Seven days
Offerings and Practices	Burnt and sin offerings. Seder meal. Eat no leavened bread. Rest, no work.	Daily offerings by fire. Eat no leavened bread. Rest, no work on 1st and 7th days.	Wave offering of sheaf of firstfruits. Burnt, grain, and wine offerings. Rest, no work.	Burnt and sin offerings. Rest, no work.	Burnt and sin offerings. Trumpet blasts.[d] Rest, no work.	Burnt, grain, and drink offerings. A complete fast. Rest, no work.	Burnt and sin offerings. Live in shelters. Rejoicing.
Scripture References	Exodus 12:1–14 Leviticus 23:5 Numbers 9:9–14; 28:16 Deuteronomy 16:1–8	Exodus 12:15–20; 13:3–10; 23:14–15 Leviticus 23:6–8 Numbers 28:17–25 Deuteronomy 16:1–8	Leviticus 23:9–14	Exodus 23:16; 34:22, 26 Leviticus 23:15–21 Numbers 28:26–31 Deuteronomy 16:9–12	Leviticus 23:23–25	Leviticus 23:26–32	Leviticus 23:33–43 Deuteronomy 16:13–17

a In addition to the Sabbath. See Leviticus 23:3.

b Because the dates are set according to the Jewish calendar, which is controlled by the phases of the moon, the dates vary from year to year in the Gregorian (today's) calendar.

c Pilgrimage festivals, meaning that all Jewish men were to come to Jerusalem to celebrate the festival. Some people consider Passover and Unleavened Bread to be one long event because they are next to each other.

d Unless it is on the Sabbath, in which case there are no trumpet blasts.

Table courtesy of The Readable Bible (www.readablebible.com)

— DAY 3 —

Today's Reading: Leviticus 22–23

Verse of the Day:

"And you shall not profane my holy name, that I may be sanctified among the people of Israel. I am the LORD who sanctifies you." — Leviticus 22:32

Questions for Reflection and Discussion

1. What type of offering did God not accept?
2. How many feasts or holy convocations are listed in this passage?

Notes on Today's Bible Reading

— DAY 4 —

Today's Reading: Leviticus 24–25

Verse of the Day:

"Therefore you shall do my statutes and keep my rules and perform them, and then you will dwell in the land securely." — Leviticus 25:18

Questions for Reflection and Discussion

1. Is the law of retaliation contained in this passage about personal vengeance or public justice?

2. This passage contains instructions for a sabbath year in which the children of Israel were to allow the land to rest—they were not to plant or harvest. If they obeyed this instruction, how would they be provided for during that year?

Notes on Today's Bible Reading

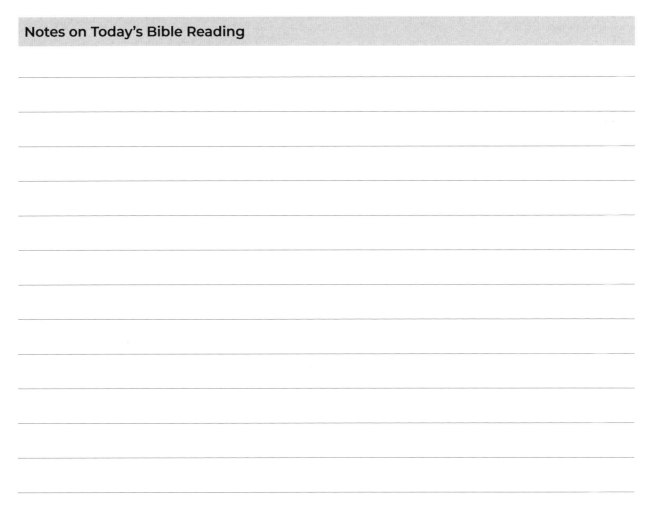

— DAY 5 —

Today's Reading: Leviticus 26–27

Verses of the Day:

"If you walk in my statutes and observe my commandments and do them, . . . I will walk among you and will be your God, and you shall be my people." — Leviticus 26:3, 12

Questions for Reflection and Discussion

1. List two of the benefits the children of Israel would experience for obeying God?

2. Were there consequences for disobeying God? If so, name two of them.

Notes on Today's Bible Reading

_____

_____

_____

_____

_____

_____

_____

_____

_____

_____

_____

_____

_____

_____

For an introduction to Numbers, see appendix 1, page 386.

— DAY 6 —

Today's Reading: Numbers 1

Verses of the Day:

"Take a census of all the congregation of the people of Israel, by clans, by fathers' houses, according to the number of names, every male, head by head. From twenty years old and upward, all in Israel who are able to go to war, you and Aaron shall list them, company by company." — Numbers 1:2–3

Questions for Reflection and Discussion

1. Who was counted in the census?
2. What tribe was not to be counted in the census?

Notes on Today's Bible Reading

— DAY 7 —
Review of This Week's Readings:
Leviticus 17–27; Numbers 1

Questions for Reflection and Discussion

1. What passage uniquely spoke to you this week?

2. What insights did you gain about God?

3. What application might this have to what is happening in the world today?

4. How would God have you apply this truth to your life?

Notes from Reflecting on This Week's Bible Readings

Have you ever made a life-altering decision you wish you could take back? Read about Israel's decision in Numbers this week.

— DAY 1 —
Today's Reading: Numbers 2–3

Verse of the Day:

"The people of Israel shall camp each by his own standard, with the banners of their fathers' houses. They shall camp facing the tent of meeting on every side." — Numbers 2:2

Questions for Reflection and Discussion

1. Were the people able to set up their tents wherever they wanted to establish their camp?

2. Why do you think they were directed to set up by family/tribe?

Notes on Today's Bible Reading

— DAY 2 —
Today's Reading: Numbers 4–5

Verse of the Day:

According to the commandment of the LORD through Moses they were listed, each one with his task of serving or carrying. Thus they were listed by him, as the LORD commanded Moses. — Numbers 4:49

Questions for Reflection and Discussion

1. How specific were the assignments given to those responsible for taking care of the tabernacle and its contents?

2. Why do you think God provided Moses with such detailed instructions?

Notes on Today's Bible Reading

— DAY 3 —

Today's Reading: Numbers 6–7

Verses of the Day:

"The LORD bless you and keep you;
the LORD make his face to shine upon you and be gracious to you;
the LORD lift up his countenance upon you and give you
peace." — Numbers 6:24–26

Questions for Reflection and Discussion

1. Why do you think God told Moses how Aaron was to bless the people?

2. What would you say characterized the gifts of the twelve leaders who brought gifts and offerings for the dedication of the altar?

Notes on Today's Bible Reading

— DAY 4 —
Today's Reading: Numbers 8–10

Verse of the Day:

And whenever the ark set out, Moses said, "Arise, O Lord, and let your enemies be scattered, and let those who hate you flee before you." — Numbers 10:35

Questions for Reflection and Discussion

1. What were the age restrictions placed on the service of the Levites?

2. What did Moses say whenever the cloud moved and the people moved out?

Notes on Today's Bible Reading

— DAY 5 —

Today's Reading: Numbers 11–12

Verse of the Day:

And the people complained in the hearing of the LORD about their misfortunes. — Numbers 11:1a

Questions for Reflection and Discussion

1. Why were the people weeping in their tents in chapter 11?

2. Why do you think Miriam, though healed, was put outside the camp for seven days?

Notes on Today's Bible Reading

— DAY 6 —

Today's Reading: Numbers 13–15

Verse of the Day:

But Caleb quieted the people before Moses and said, "Let us go up at once and occupy it, for we are well able to overcome it." — Numbers 13:30

Questions for Reflection and Discussion

1. After Joshua and Caleb returned from spying out the promised land, what did they tell the people *not* to do?

2. What was the purpose of the tassels on their garments?

Notes on Today's Bible Reading

— DAY 7 —
Review of This Week's Readings:
Numbers 2–15

Questions for Reflection and Discussion

1. What passage uniquely spoke to you this week?

2. What insights did you gain about God?

3. What application might this have to what is happening in the world today?

4. How would God have you apply this truth to your life?

Notes from Reflecting on This Week's Bible Readings

Week 12

What actionable attitude stands out before God and receives His reward? Find out as we continue the book of Numbers.

— DAY 1 —
Today's Reading: Numbers 16–17

Verse of the Day:

And he [Aaron] stood between the dead and the living, and the plague was stopped. — Numbers 16:48

Questions for Reflection and Discussion

1. What caused the plague to break out among the congregation?

2. Aaron put incense in the censer and stood between the people and the plague. What did the incense represent?

Notes on Today's Bible Reading

— DAY 2 —

Today's Reading: Numbers 18–19

Verse of the Day:

"I give your priesthood as a gift." — Numbers 18:7b

Questions for Reflection and Discussion

1. Aaron and his sons' ability to serve as priests was considered a _____ from God.
   a. Task
   b. Burden
   c. Gift
   d. None of the above

2. What was the purpose of the red heifer sacrifice?

Notes on Today's Bible Reading

— DAY 3 —

Today's Reading: Numbers 20–21

Verse of the Day:

And the Lord said to Moses and Aaron, "Because you did not believe in me, to uphold me as holy in the eyes of the people of Israel, therefore you shall not bring this assembly into the land that I have given them." — Numbers 20:12

Questions for Reflection and Discussion

1. Moses sinned by striking the rock rather than speaking to it as God had instructed. As a result, Moses and Aaron were not permitted to go into the promised land. What does this tell us about sin, even when we are forgiven?

2. What did the bronze serpent set on a pole represent, which those bitten looked to for healing?

Notes on Today's Bible Reading

— DAY 4 —

Today's Reading: Numbers 22–23

Verses of the Day:

"How can I curse whom God has not cursed?

How can I denounce whom the LORD has not denounced? . . .

[H]e has blessed, and I cannot revoke it." — Numbers 23:8, 20

Questions for Reflection and Discussion

1. Who opposed the efforts of Balaam to curse the children of Israel?

2. What happened when Balaam opened his mouth to curse the children of Israel?

Notes on Today's Bible Reading

— DAY 5 —
Today's Reading: Numbers 24–25

Verse of the Day:

"Phinehas the son of Eleazar, son of Aaron the priest, has turned back my wrath from the people of Israel, in that he was jealous with my jealousy among them, so that I did not consume the people of Israel in my jealousy." — Numbers 25:11

Questions for Reflection and Discussion

1. What did the children of Israel do to arouse the anger of the Lord?
2. What was Phinehas' reward for taking action and stopping the plague?

Notes on Today's Bible Reading

— DAY 6 —
Today's Reading: Numbers 26

Verse of the Day:

"Take a census of all the congregation of the people of Israel, from twenty years old and upward, by their fathers' houses, all in Israel who are able to go to war." — Numbers 26:2

Questions for Reflection and Discussion

1. What was the purpose of the census?

2. Who was left of the original twelve spies who went into the promised land forty years before?

Notes on Today's Bible Reading

— DAY 7 —
Review of This Week's Readings:
Numbers 16–26

Questions for Reflection and Discussion

1. What passage uniquely spoke to you this week?

2. What insights did you gain about God?

3. What application might this have to what is happening in the world today?

4. How would God have you apply this truth to your life?

Notes from Reflecting on This Week's Bible Readings

Why should we be careful as Christians about who we allow to influence us? Find out as we conclude Numbers this week.

— DAY 1 —

Today's Reading: Numbers 27–28

Verses of the Day:

"Let the LORD, the God of the spirits of all flesh, appoint a man over the congregation who shall go out before them and come in before them, who shall lead them out and bring them in, that the congregation of the LORD may not be as sheep that have no shepherd." — Numbers 27:16–17

Questions for Reflection and Discussion

1. What did the daughters of Zelophehad want permission to do from Moses?

2. What did God say about Joshua when He told Moses to take Joshua and set him before Eleazar and the people?

Notes on Today's Bible Reading

— DAY 2 —

Today's Reading: Numbers 29–30

Verse of the Day:

"If a man vows a vow to the LORD, or swears an oath to bind himself by a pledge, he shall not break his word. He shall do according to all that proceeds out of his mouth." — Numbers 30:2

Questions for Reflection and Discussion

1. On the Day of Atonement, the tenth day of the seventh month, the children of Israel were to do which of the following?
    a. Gather in a holy convocation
    b. Fast
    c. Not work
    d. All the above

2. What was required of those who made a vow?

Notes on Today's Bible Reading

— DAY 3 —

Today's Reading: Numbers 31–32

Verses of the Day:

The LORD spoke to Moses, saying, "Avenge the people of Israel on the Midianites. Afterward you shall be gathered to your people." — Numbers 31:1–2

Questions for Reflection and Discussion

1. Why were the children ordered to take vengeance on the Midianites?

2. What did Moses say would happen if the tribes of Reuben and Gad did not keep their word, cross over the Jordan, and help take the promised land?

Notes on Today's Bible Reading

_____

_____

_____

_____

_____

_____

_____

_____

_____

_____

_____

_____

_____

— DAY 4 —
Today's Reading: Numbers 33–34

Verse of the Day:

"And you shall take possession of the land and settle in it, for I have given the land to you to possess it." — Numbers 33:53

Questions for Reflection and Discussion

1. Why did Moses keep a record of each time God had the children of Israel move during their forty–year journey?

2. What did God say would be the consequences of the children of Israel failing to eliminate the influence of those who occupied the land they were entering?

Notes on Today's Bible Reading

— DAY 5 —
Today's Reading: Numbers 35–36

Verse of the Day:

"You shall not defile the land in which you live, in the midst of which I dwell, for I the LORD dwell in the midst of the people of Israel." — Numbers 35:34

Questions for Reflection and Discussion

1. How many cities of refuge were established?

2. What was the purpose of these cities of refuge?

Notes on Today's Bible Reading

For an introduction to Deuteronomy, see appendix 1, page 387.

— DAY 6 —

Today's Reading: Deuteronomy 1–2

Verses of the Day:

"Then I said to you, 'Do not be in dread or afraid of them. The Lord your God who goes before you will himself fight for you, just as he did for you in Egypt before your eyes.'" — Deuteronomy 1:29–30

Questions for Reflection and Discussion

1. What qualities did Moses tell the people to look for in the leaders they selected?

2. What was the key to judges not being afraid of any man in their decisions?

Notes on Today's Bible Reading

— DAY 7 —
Review of This Week's Readings:
Numbers 27–36; Deuteronomy 1–2

Questions for Reflection and Discussion

1. What passage uniquely spoke to you this week?

2. What insights did you gain about God?

3. What application might this have to what is happening in the world today?

4. How would God have you apply this truth to your life?

Notes from Reflecting on This Week's Bible Readings

_____

_____

_____

_____

_____

_____

_____

_____

_____

_____

_____

_____

_____

_____

_____

What is our God-given responsibility toward our children? Find out this week as we continue in Deuteronomy.

— DAY 1 —

Today's Reading: Deuteronomy 3–4

Verse of the Day:

"Only take care, and keep your soul diligently, lest you forget the things that your eyes have seen, and lest they depart from your heart all the days of your life. Make them known to your children and your children's children." — Deuteronomy 4:9

Questions for Reflection and Discussion

1. What did God say to Moses when he pleaded with God to allow him to cross over the Jordan and see the promised land?

2. Moses pointed the Israelites to what as the source of their wisdom and understanding as a nation?

Notes on Today's Bible Reading

— DAY 2 —

Today's Reading: Deuteronomy 5–7

Verses of the Day:

"You shall love the LORD your God with all your heart and with all your soul and with all your might. And these words that I command you today shall be on your heart. You shall teach them diligently to your children, and shall talk of them when you sit in your house, and when you walk by the way, and when you lie down, and when you rise." — Deuteronomy 6:5–7

Questions for Reflection and Discussion

1. Does spiritual idolatry by one generation affect subsequent generations?

2. How does this passage say we can secure our future and our children's futures?

Notes on Today's Bible Reading

— DAY 3 —

Today's Reading: Deuteronomy 8–10

Verse of the Day:

"And you shall remember the whole way that the Lord your God has led you these forty years in the wilderness, that he might humble you, testing you to know what was in your heart, whether you would keep his commandments or not." — Deuteronomy 8:2

Questions for Reflection and Discussion

1. What was the purpose of the wilderness experience?
2. What does this passage say is required to follow the Lord?

Notes on Today's Bible Reading

— DAY 4 —

Today's Reading: Deuteronomy 11–12

Verse of the Day:

"Be careful to obey all these words that I command you, that it may go well with you and with your children after you forever, when you do what is good and right in the sight of the LORD your God." — Deuteronomy 12:28

Questions for Reflection and Discussion

1. What does this passage say diligent obedience brings?
2. What choice did God give to the people?

Notes on Today's Bible Reading

— DAY 5 —

Today's Reading: Deuteronomy 13–15

Verse of the Day:

"You shall walk after the LORD your God and fear him and keep his commandments and obey his voice, and you shall serve him and hold fast to him." — Deuteronomy 13:4

Questions for Reflection and Discussion

1. This passage talks about a third-year tithe. How was it to be used?

2. What would be the result of using this tithe as God directed?

Notes on Today's Bible Reading

— DAY 6 —

Today's Reading: Deuteronomy 16–19

Verse of the Day:

"The LORD your God will raise up for you a prophet like me from among you, from your brothers—it is to him you shall listen." — Deuteronomy 18:15

Questions for Reflection and Discussion

1. What are the effects of bribes?

2. Name two reasons God states in this passage that the inhabitants of the land were being driven out before the children of Israel.

Notes on Today's Bible Reading

— DAY 7 —
Review of This Week's Readings:
Deuteronomy 3–19

Questions for Reflection and Discussion

1. What passage uniquely spoke to you this week?

2. What insights did you gain about God?

3. What application might this have to what is happening in the world today?

4. How would God have you apply this truth to your life?

Notes from Reflecting on This Week's Bible Readings

Week 15

How can we ensure success as Christians? Find out this week as we finish Deuteronomy and start the book of Joshua.

— DAY 1 —

Today's Reading: Deuteronomy 20–22

Verse of the Day:

"You shall not see your brother's ox or his sheep going astray and ignore them. You shall take them back to your brother."
— Deuteronomy 22:1

Questions for Reflection and Discussion

1. What did God say the Israelites should *not* do when they go out to battle against a physically superior army?

2. What are you supposed to do if you find something that belongs to your "brother" or neighbor?

Notes on Today's Bible Reading

— DAY 2 —

Today's Reading: Deuteronomy 23–26

Verse of the Day:

"[H]e will set you in praise and in fame and in honor high above all nations that he has made, and that you shall be a people holy to the LORD your God, as he promised." — Deuteronomy 26:19

Questions for Reflection and Discussion

1. What did God do when Balaam attempted to curse the children of Israel and why?

2. Why was someone prohibited from taking the lower or upper millstone in a financial pledge?

Notes on Today's Bible Reading

— DAY 3 —

Today's Reading: Deuteronomy 27–28

Verses of the Day:

"The Lord will command the blessing on you in your barns and in all that you undertake. . . . The Lord will establish you as a people holy to himself, as he has sworn to you, if you keep the commandments of the Lord your God and walk in his ways. And all the peoples of the earth shall see that you are called by the name of the Lord, and they shall be afraid of you."
— Deuteronomy 28:8a, 9b–10

Questions for Reflection and Discussion

1. In what manner would the blessings of God come to those who obeyed Him?

2. What were the conditions of receiving the blessing of God?

Notes on Today's Bible Reading

— DAY 4 —

Today's Reading: Deuteronomy 29–30

Verse of the Day:

"I call heaven and earth to witness against you today, that I have set before you life and death, blessing and curse. Therefore choose life, that you and your offspring may live." — Deuteronomy 30:19

Questions for Reflection and Discussion

1. If the "secret things" belong to the Lord, what things belong to us and what is their purpose (29:29)?

2. When God sent His rebellious people into exile, what was the remedy and His promise (30:1–10)?

Notes on Today's Bible Reading

— DAY 5 —

Today's Reading: Deuteronomy 31–34

Verse of the Day:

"Be strong and courageous. Do not fear or be in dread of them, for it is the Lord your God who goes with you. He will not leave you or forsake you." — Deuteronomy 31:6

Questions for Reflection and Discussion

1. What was Moses's final public act before his death?

2. While God did not allow Moses to enter the promised land, what did God allow Moses to do on Mount Nebo before his death?

Notes on Today's Bible Reading

For an introduction to Joshua, see appendix 1, page 388.

— DAY 6 —

Today's Reading: Joshua 1–3

Verse of the Day:

"Only be strong and very courageous, being careful to do according to all the law that Moses my servant commanded you. Do not turn from it to the right hand or to the left, that you may have good success wherever you go." — Joshua 1:7

Questions for Reflection and Discussion

1. What did God say Joshua's success was dependent upon?

2. What specifically caused the hearts of the people of Jericho to melt in fear before the Israelites crossed the Jordan River?

Notes on Today's Bible Reading

— DAY 7 —

Review of This Week's Readings:
Deuteronomy 20–34; Joshua 1–3

Questions for Reflection and Discussion

1. What passage uniquely spoke to you this week?

2. What insights did you gain about God?

3. What application might this have to what is happening in the world today?

4. How would God have you apply this truth to your life?

Notes from Reflecting on This Week's Bible Readings

_____

_____

_____

_____

_____

_____

_____

_____

_____

_____

_____

_____

_____

_____

_____

What happens when we do not seek the Lord's counsel before making important decisions? Find out this week as we continue reading in the book of Joshua.

— DAY 1 —

Today's Reading: Joshua 4–5

Verse of the Day:

"[A]nd command them, saying, 'Take twelve stones from here out of the midst of the Jordan, from the very place where the priests' feet stood firmly, and bring them over with you and lay them down in the place where you lodge tonight.'" — Joshua 4:3

Questions for Reflection and Discussion

1. After God stopped the raging waters of the Jordan River so that the people could cross on dry ground, why did He command a stone monument be built?

2. What was Joshua's response to the commander of the Lord's army?

Notes on Today's Bible Reading

_____

_____

_____

_____

_____

_____

_____

_____

_____

_____

— DAY 2 —
Today's Reading: Joshua 6–8

Verse of the Day:

"Get up! Consecrate the people and say, 'Consecrate yourselves for tomorrow; for thus says the LORD, God of Israel, "There are devoted things in your midst, O Israel. You cannot stand before your enemies until you take away the devoted things from among you."'"
— Joshua 7:13

Questions for Reflection and Discussion

1. Why was Israel defeated when they first went up against Ai?

2. After the victory at Ai, what did Joshua do with the Israelites at Mount Ebal?

Notes on Today's Bible Reading

— DAY 3 —
Today's Reading: Joshua 9–10

Verse of the Day:

"There has been no day like it before or since, when the LORD heeded the voice of a man, for the LORD fought for Israel." — Joshua 10:14

Questions for Reflection and Discussion

1. How did the Gibeonites trick Joshua and the leaders into a costly alliance?

2. What did God do to give Joshua time to gain a complete victory over the Amorites?

Notes on Today's Bible Reading

— DAY 4 —

Today's Reading: Joshua 11–12

Verse of the Day:

"So Joshua took the whole land, according to all that the Lord had spoken to Moses. And Joshua gave it for an inheritance to Israel according to their tribal allotments. And the land had rest from war." — Joshua 11:23

Questions for Reflection and Discussion

1. What did the Lord tell Joshua when all the kings and their armies met at the waters of Merom to fight against Israel?

2. Why did Joshua and the Israelites not battle the Hivites?

Notes on Today's Bible Reading

— DAY 5 —

Today's Reading: Joshua 13–14

Verse of the Day:

"And Moses swore on that day, saying, 'Surely the land on which your foot has trodden shall be an inheritance for you and your children forever, because you have wholly followed the Lᴏʀᴅ my God.'" — Joshua 14:9

Questions for Reflection and Discussion

1. What was the basis for Moses' promise to Caleb that the land he had walked on would be his and his children's inheritance?

2. What was Caleb relying upon to drive the Anakim out of the land?

Notes on Today's Bible Reading

— DAY 6 —

Today's Reading: Joshua 15

Verse of the Day:

"According to the commandment of the LORD to Joshua, he gave to Caleb the son of Jephunneh a portion among the people of Judah, Kiriath-arba, that is, Hebron (Arba was the father of Anak)." — Joshua 15:13

Questions for Reflection and Discussion

1. What was promised to the man who conquered Kiriath-sepher?
2. What did Caleb's daughter ask for?

Notes on Today's Bible Reading

— DAY 7 —
Review of This Week's Readings:
Joshua 4–15

Questions for Reflection and Discussion

1. What passage uniquely spoke to you this week?

2. What insights did you gain about God?

3. What application might this have to what is happening in the world today?

4. How would God have you apply this truth to your life?

Notes from Reflecting on This Week's Bible Readings

Week 17

What declaration should all Christians make as leaders in the home? Find out as we conclude our study of Joshua.

— DAY 1 —

Today's Reading: Joshua 16–18

Verse of the Day:

Now when the people of Israel grew strong, they put the Canaanites to forced labor, but did not utterly drive them out. — Joshua 17:13

Questions for Reflection and Discussion

1. Because the tribe of Manasseh was unable to drive out the Canaanites, what did they ultimately do with them?

2. At this point, how many tribes had not yet taken possession of the land that was given to them?

Notes on Today's Bible Reading

_____

_____

_____

_____

_____

_____

_____

_____

_____

_____

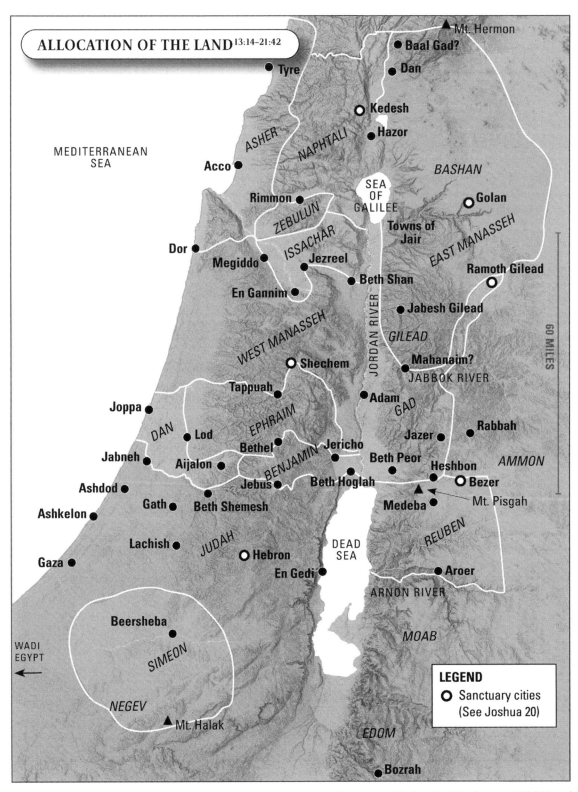

ALLOCATION OF THE LAND 13:14–21:42

▲ Mt. Hermon
Baal Gad?
Dan
○ Kedesh
Tyre
Hazor
ASHER
NAPHTALI
MEDITERRANEAN SEA
BASHAN
Acco
SEA OF GALILEE
Rimmon
ZEBULUN
Golan ○
ISSACHAR
Towns of Jair
EAST MANASSEH
Dor
Megiddo
Jezreel
Ramoth Gilead ○
En Gannim
Beth Shan
Jabesh Gilead
WEST MANASSEH
GILEAD
JORDAN RIVER
Mahanaim?
Shechem ○
JABBOK RIVER
Tappuah
Joppa
Adam
GAD
DAN
Lod
EPHRAIM
Jazer
Rabbah
Bethel
Jericho
Bethel
BENJAMIN
Beth Peor
Jabneh
Aijalon
Heshbon
AMMON
Jebus
Beth Hoglah
Bezer ○
Ashdod
▲ Mt. Pisgah
Gath
Beth Shemesh
Medeba
Ashkelon
Lachish
JUDAH
DEAD SEA
REUBEN
Gaza
Hebron ○
En Gedi
Aroer
ARNON RIVER
WADI EGYPT
MOAB
Beersheba
SIMEON
NEGEV
▲ Mt. Halak
EDOM
Bozrah

60 MILES

LEGEND
○ Sanctuary cities
(See Joshua 20)

Map courtesy of The Readable Bible (www.readablebible.com)

— DAY 2 —

Today's Reading: Joshua 19

Verse of the Day:

These are the inheritances that Eleazar the priest and Joshua the son of Nun and the heads of the fathers' houses of the tribes of the people of Israel distributed by lot at Shiloh before the LORD, at the entrance of the tent of meeting. So they finished dividing the land. — Joshua 19:51

Questions for Reflection and Discussion

1. What tribe drew the seventh lot?
2. Where did Joshua, Eleazar, and other leaders draw the lots?

Notes on Today's Bible Reading

— DAY 3 —
Today's Reading: Joshua 20–21

Verse of the Day:

Not one word of all the good promises that the Lord had made to the house of Israel had failed; all came to pass. — Joshua 21:45

Questions for Reflection and Discussion

1. What was the purpose of the cities of refuge?
2. How many cities were given to the Levites?

Notes on Today's Bible Reading

— DAY 4 —

Today's Reading: Joshua 22–23

Verse of the Day:

"Therefore, be very strong to keep and to do all that is written in the Book of the Law of Moses, turning aside from it neither to the right hand nor to the left." — Joshua 23:6

Questions for Reflection and Discussion

1. Why did the Israelites on the west side of the Jordan become upset when they heard the tribes of Reuben, Gad, and Manasseh built an altar on the other side of the Jordan?

2. As a part of his final address to the leaders, Joshua told them to be very courageous and do what?

Notes on Today's Bible Reading

— DAY 5 —

Today's Reading: Joshua 24

Verse of the Day:

"And if it is evil in your eyes to serve the LORD, choose this day whom you will serve, whether the gods your fathers served in the region beyond the River, or the gods of the Amorites in whose land you dwell. But as for me and my house, we will serve the LORD." — Joshua 24:15

Questions for Reflection and Discussion

1. In his final words to the people, Joshua told them to:
   a. Fear the Lord
   b. Serve the Lord
   c. Reject idolatry
   d. None of the above
   e. All of the above

2. What declaration did Joshua make that displayed his godly leadership in his home?

Notes on Today's Bible Reading

For an introduction to Judges, see appendix 1, page 389.

— DAY 6 —

Today's Reading: Judges 1–2

Verse of the Day:

And the people of Israel did what was evil in the sight of the LORD and served the Baals. — Judges 2:11

Questions for Reflection and Discussion

1. What happened when a generation grew up not knowing the Lord or the work He had done in Israel's history?

2. What happened to Israel's strength and security when they forsook God and followed the gods of the people who were around them?

Notes on Today's Bible Reading

— DAY 7 —
Review of This Week's Readings:
Joshua 16–24; Judges 1–2

Questions for Reflection and Discussion

1. What passage uniquely spoke to you this week?

2. What insights did you gain about God?

3. What application might this have to what is happening in the world today?

4. How would God have you apply this truth to your life?

Notes from Reflecting on This Week's Bible Readings

Week 18

Why is having God on our side more important than having numbers on our side? Find out this week as we continue the book of Judges.

— DAY 1 —
Today's Reading: Judges 3–4

Verse of the Day:

But when the people of Israel cried out to the Lord, the Lord raised up a deliverer for the people of Israel, who saved them. — Judges 3:9a

Questions for Reflection and Discussion

1. As a result of Israel's sin, whom did God strengthen to oppress Israel?

2. Ehud told King Eglon that he had a message from whom?

Notes on Today's Bible Reading

— DAY 2 —

Today's Reading: Judges 5–6

Verse of the Day:

"So may all your enemies perish, O Lᴏʀᴅ!
 But your friends be like the sun as he rises in his might."
And the land had rest for forty years. — Judges 5:31

Questions for Reflection and Discussion

1. What was the result in Israel when Deborah provided leadership?

2. In the account of Gideon, how do we see the substance of evil being used for God's purposes?

Notes on Today's Bible Reading

— DAY 3 —

Today's Reading: Judges 7–8

Verse of the Day:

The LORD said to Gideon, "The people with you are too many for me to give the Midianites into their hand, lest Israel boast over me, saying, 'My own hand has saved me.'" — Judges 7:2

Questions for Reflection and Discussion

1. Why do you think the three hundred men who stayed on their feet and brought water to their mouths were the ones chosen to be in Gideon's army?

2. What mistake did Gideon make with the gold from the kings of Midian?

Notes on Today's Bible Reading

— DAY 4 —

Today's Reading: Judges 9

Verse of the Day:

But there was a strong tower within the city, and all the men and women and all the leaders of the city fled to it and shut themselves in, and they went up to the roof of the tower. — Judges 9:51

Questions for Reflection and Discussion

1. Did the people of Israel honor or dishonor Gideon (Jerubbaal) after his death?

2. How did evil Abimelech meet his end, and who was responsible for his death?

Notes on Today's Bible Reading

— DAY 5 —
Today's Reading: Judges 10–11

Verse of the Day:

And the people, the leaders of Gilead, said one to another, "Who is the man who will begin to fight against the Ammonites? He shall be head over all the inhabitants of Gilead." — Judges 10:18

Questions for Reflection and Discussion

1. Why did the elders and the people of Gilead make Jephthah commander over them?
2. What vow did Jephthah make to the Lord?

Notes on Today's Bible Reading

— DAY 6 —
Today's Reading: Judges 12–14

Verse of the Day:

And the people of Israel again did what was evil in the sight of the LORD, so the LORD gave them into the hand of the Philistines for forty years. — Judges 13:1

Questions for Reflection and Discussion

1. After Jephthah and the Gileadites defeated the Ephraimites, how were they able to determine who among the survivors were Ephraimites and who were not?

2. After the angel of the Lord foretold Samson's birth, what did Manoah ask the Lord?

Notes on Today's Bible Reading

— DAY 7 —
Review of This Week's Readings:
Judges 3–14

Questions for Reflection and Discussion

1. What passage uniquely spoke to you this week?

2. What insights did you gain about God?

3. What application might this have to what is happening in the world today?

4. How would God have you apply this truth to your life?

Notes from Reflecting on This Week's Bible Readings

Week 19

Today, many people want to live their own truth, but what happened when the people of Israel did that? Find out as we finish studying in Judges.

— DAY 1 —

Today's Reading: Judges 15–16

Verse of the Day:

When he came to Lehi, the Philistines came shouting to meet him. Then the Spirit of the LORD rushed upon him, and the ropes that were on his arms became as flax that has caught fire, and his bonds melted off his hands. — Judges 15:14

Questions for Reflection and Discussion

1. What was the secret of Samson's strength?
2. What was Samson's final act?

Notes on Today's Bible Reading

— DAY 2 —

Today's Reading: Judges 17–18

Verse of the Day:

In those days there was no king in Israel. Everyone did what was right in his own eyes. — Judges 17:6

Questions for Reflection and Discussion

1. What did Micah confess to his mother?

2. When the five Danite warriors came across the Levite priest, what did they ask of him?

Notes on Today's Bible Reading

— DAY 3 —

Today's Reading: Judges 19

Verse of the Day:

And all who saw it said, "Such a thing has never happened or been seen from the day that the people of Israel came up out of the land of Egypt until this day; consider it, take counsel, and speak." — Judges 19:30

Questions for Reflection and Discussion

1. What did the wicked men of Gibeah demand?

2. When a nation and a people depart from God and sink to such lows of idolatry and immorality, what is the result for the value of a human life?

Notes on Today's Bible Reading

_____

_____

_____

_____

_____

_____

_____

_____

_____

_____

_____

_____

— DAY 4 —

Today's Reading: Judges 20–21

Verse of the Day:

And the people of Israel inquired of the Lord. — Judges 20:27a

Questions for Reflection and Discussion

1. What was the cause of the horrible civil war between Israel and the tribe of Benjamin?

2. Who served as high priest and inquired of the Lord on behalf of Israel?

Notes on Today's Bible Reading

_____

_____

_____

_____

_____

_____

_____

_____

_____

_____

_____

_____

_____

_____

_____

_____

_____

For an introduction
to Ruth,
see appendix 1,
page 390.

— DAY 5 —

Today's Reading: Ruth 1–2

Verse of the Day:

Then she fell on her face, bowing to the ground, and said to him, "Why have I found favor in your eyes, that you should take notice of me, since I am a foreigner?" — Ruth 2:10

Questions for Reflection and Discussion

1. What did Ruth say about Naomi's God?

2. What is the difference between Israel's provision for the poor and our current welfare system?

Notes on Today's Bible Reading

— DAY 6 —

Today's Reading: Ruth 3–4

Verse of the Day:

Then the women said to Naomi, "Blessed be the LORD, who has not left you this day without a redeemer, and may his name be renowned in Israel!" — Ruth 4:14

Questions for Reflection and Discussion

1. Regarding Ruth's prospects of getting remarried, how did Naomi's attitude change since the first chapter?

2. How is Boaz and what he did for Ruth a picture of what Jesus has done for us?

Notes on Today's Bible Reading

— DAY 7 —
Review of This Week's Readings:
Judges 15–21; Ruth 1–4

Questions for Reflection and Discussion

1. What passage uniquely spoke to you this week?

2. What insights did you gain about God?

3. What application might this have to what is happening in the world today?

4. How would God have you apply this truth to your life?

Notes from Reflecting on This Week's Bible Readings

Week 20

How should we respond to God's calling on our lives? Find out as we begin 1 Samuel this week.

For an introduction to 1 Samuel, see appendix 1, page 392.

— DAY 1 —

Today's Reading: 1 Samuel 1–2

Verse of the Day:

"For this child I prayed, and the LORD has granted me my petition that I made to him." — 1 Samuel 1:27

Questions for Reflection and Discussion

1. What do Hannah's prayers tell us about how she understood God?
2. What did Eli do about his sons' sinful behavior as priests, and how did they respond?

Notes on Today's Bible Reading

— DAY 2 —

Today's Reading: 1 Samuel 3–5

Verse of the Day:

And she named the child Ichabod, saying, "The glory has departed from Israel!" because the ark of God had been captured and because of her father-in-law and her husband. — 1 Samuel 4:21

Questions for Reflection and Discussion

1. What did Eli coach young Samuel to say to God when He called?

2. What does the story about the capture of the ark of the covenant teach us? Is it possible to feel confident God is on our side when He is not?

Notes on Today's Bible Reading

— DAY 3 —

Today's Reading: 1 Samuel 6–8

Verse of the Day:

Then the men of Beth-shemesh said, "Who is able to stand before the Lord, this holy God? And to whom shall he go up away from us?" — 1 Samuel 6:20

Questions for Reflection and Discussion

1. What test did the Philistines design to determine if the God of Israel was behind the plague that broke out among them?

2. What did Samuel prescribe as the way of deliverance from the oppression of the Philistines?

Notes on Today's Bible Reading

— DAY 4 —

Today's Reading: 1 Samuel 9–10

Verse of the Day:

And he had a son whose name was Saul, a handsome young man. There was not a man among the people of Israel more handsome than he. From his shoulders upward he was taller than any of the people. — 1 Samuel 9:2

Questions for Reflection and Discussion

1. What did Samuel tell Saul would happen, and what did happen that prepared Saul to become the leader of Israel?

2. What caused the valiant men to follow Saul?

Notes on Today's Bible Reading

— DAY 5 —

Today's Reading: 1 Samuel 11–13

Verse of the Day:

"Only fear the L ORD and serve him faithfully with all your heart. For consider what great things he has done for you." — 1 Samuel 12:24

Questions for Reflection and Discussion

1. What stirred up the anger of Saul over the threat to the people of Jabesh?

2. What did Samuel tell the people to do if they did not want to be swept away by God for doing wickedness?

Notes on Today's Bible Reading

— DAY 6 —
Today's Reading: 1 Samuel 14

Verse of the Day:

Jonathan said to the young man who carried his armor, "Come, let us go over to the garrison of these uncircumcised. It may be that the LORD will work for us, for nothing can hinder the LORD from saving by many or by few." — 1 Samuel 14:6

Questions for Reflection and Discussion

1. Jonathan's confidence that he and his armorbearer could successfully take on a more significant number of Philistines was based upon:
   a. His and his armorbearer's ability
   b. A dream that he had
   c. The power of God
   d. All the above

2. What does this passage teach us about making vows or oaths?

Notes on Today's Bible Reading

— DAY 7 —
Review of This Week's Readings:
1 Samuel 1–14

Questions for Reflection and Discussion

1. What passage uniquely spoke to you this week?

2. What insights did you gain about God?

3. What application might this have to what is happening in the world today?

4. How would God have you apply this truth to your life?

Notes from Reflecting on This Week's Bible Readings

How can we prevail when facing a huge challenge? Find out as we read about David in 1 Samuel this week.

— DAY 1 —

Today's Reading: 1 Samuel 15–16

Verse of the Day:

And Samuel said to him, "The LORD has torn the kingdom of Israel from you this day and has given it to a neighbor of yours, who is better than you." — 1 Samuel 15:28

Questions for Reflection and Discussion

1. What two glaring leadership failures did Saul display in what he did following the attack on the Amalekites?

2. What did Samuel say about God's view of obedience?

Notes on Today's Bible Reading

— DAY 2 —

Today's Reading: 1 Samuel 17

Verse of the Day:

Then David said to the Philistine, "You come to me with a sword and with a spear and with a javelin, but I come to you in the name of the Lord of hosts, the God of the armies of Israel, whom you have defied." — 1 Samuel 17:45

Questions for Reflection and Discussion

1. How did Saul and his army react to Goliath's challenge?

2. What can we learn from David's decision regarding Saul's armor?

Notes on Today's Bible Reading

— DAY 3 —

Today's Reading: 1 Samuel 18–19

Verse of the Day:

And Saul was very angry, and this saying displeased him. He said, "They have ascribed to David ten thousands, and to me they have ascribed thousands, and what more can he have but the kingdom?" — 1 Samuel 18:8

Questions for Reflection and Discussion

1. What prompted Saul to eye David with suspicion and jealousy?
2. What happened to the men Saul sent to Naioth to capture David?

Notes on Today's Bible Reading

— DAY 4 —

Today's Reading: 1 Samuel 20–21

Verse of the Day:

And David rose and fled that day from Saul and went to Achish the king of Gath. — 1 Samuel 21:10

Questions for Reflection and Discussion

1. When Jonathan told the lad, "the arrows are beyond you," what was he communicating to David?

2. What did David do in Gath when he became afraid that Achish might take revenge on him?

Notes on Today's Bible Reading

— DAY 5 —

Today's Reading: 1 Samuel 22–23

Verse of the Day:

And Jonathan, Saul's son, rose and went to David at Horesh, and strengthened his hand in God. — 1 Samuel 23:16

Questions for Reflection and Discussion

1. What kind of men joined David at the cave of Adullam?
   a. Successful
   b. Prosperous
   c. Desperate
   d. All the above

2. Saul sought David every day, but why could he not find him?

Notes on Today's Bible Reading

— DAY 6 —

Today's Reading: 1 Samuel 24–25

Verse of the Day:

"May the LORD therefore be judge and give sentence between me and you, and see to it and plead my cause and deliver me from your hand." — 1 Samuel 24:15

Questions for Reflection and Discussion

1. What did David's men suggest God was doing when Saul came into the cave where they were hiding?

2. What did Abigail's wise appeal keep David from doing?

Notes on Today's Bible Reading

_____

_____

_____

_____

_____

_____

_____

_____

_____

_____

_____

_____

— DAY 7 —
Review of This Week's Readings:
1 Samuel 15–25

Questions for Reflection and Discussion

1. What passage uniquely spoke to you this week?

2. What insights did you gain about God?

3. What application might this have to what is happening in the world today?

4. How would God have you apply this truth to your life?

Notes from Reflecting on This Week's Bible Readings

Week 22

Should we show respect to leaders when they are morally corrupt? Learn from David and Saul in 1 Samuel.

— DAY 1 —

Today's Reading: 1 Samuel 26–28

Verse of the Day:

"Behold, as your life was precious this day in my sight, so may my life be precious in the sight of the Lord, and may he deliver me out of all tribulation." — 1 Samuel 26:24

Questions for Reflection and Discussion

1. Why didn't Saul and his men wake up when David and Abishai were walking in their camp?

2. Why do you think Saul was so afraid when he saw the army of the Philistines?

Notes on Today's Bible Reading

— DAY 2 —

Today's Reading: 1 Samuel 29–31

Verse of the Day:

And David was greatly distressed, for the people spoke of stoning him, because all the people were bitter in soul, each for his sons and daughters. But David strengthened himself in the LORD his God. — 1 Samuel 30:6

Questions for Reflection and Discussion

1. Achish dismissed David because the Philistine kings were afraid he might join Saul and turn against them, but why do you think God may have used their concern to remove David from this battle?

2. In the wake of the attack on Ziklag and David's men turning on him in distress, how did David find the strength to continue?

Notes on Today's Bible Reading

For an introduction to 2 Samuel, see appendix 1, page 393.

— DAY 3 —

Today's Reading: 2 Samuel 1–2

Verse of the Day:

And David lamented with this lamentation over Saul and Jonathan his son. — 2 Samuel 1:17

Questions for Reflection and Discussion

1. What does David's reaction to Saul's death reveal about David?

2. In what city did David reign as king of Judah?

Notes on Today's Bible Reading

— DAY 4 —

Today's Reading: 2 Samuel 3–4

Verse of the Day:

There was a long war between the house of Saul and the house of David. And David grew stronger and stronger, while the house of Saul became weaker and weaker. — 2 Samuel 3:1

Questions for Reflection and Discussion

1. How did David respond to the death of Abner?

2. What did David do for those who executed Ishbosheth and brought him Ishbosheth's head?

Notes on Today's Bible Reading

— DAY 5 —

Today's Reading: 2 Samuel 5–7

Verse of the Day:

"When your days are fulfilled and you lie down with your fathers, I will raise up your offspring after you, who shall come from your body, and I will establish his kingdom." — 2 Samuel 7:12

Questions for Reflection and Discussion

1. After David became king over all of Israel, the _____ was brought to Jerusalem.
   a. Throne
   b. Ark
   c. Goliath's sword
   d. The tabernacle
2. What did David do before the Lord that made Michal mad?

Notes on Today's Bible Reading

_____

_____

_____

_____

_____

_____

_____

_____

_____

_____

_____

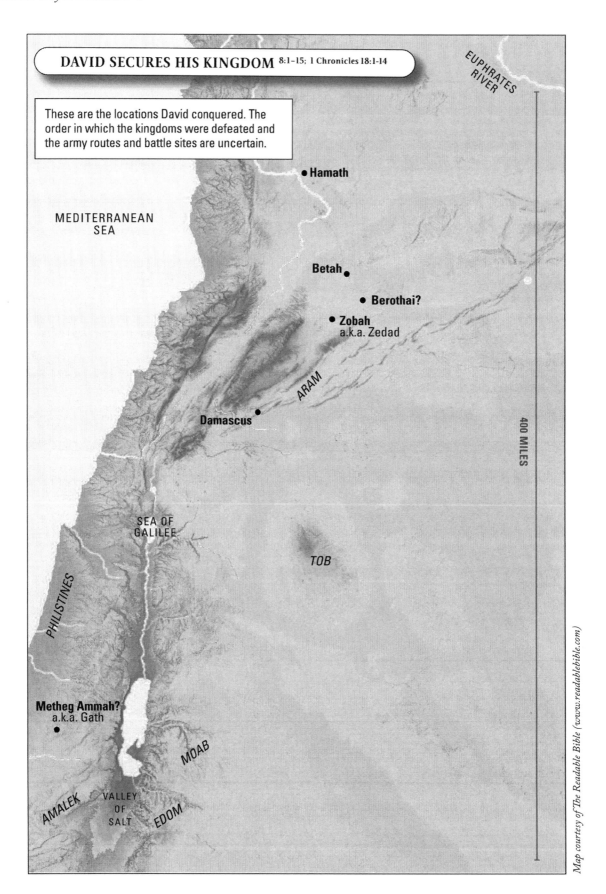

DAVID SECURES HIS KINGDOM 8:1–15; 1 Chronicles 18:1-14

These are the locations David conquered. The order in which the kingdoms were defeated and the army routes and battle sites are uncertain.

EUPHRATES RIVER

● Hamath

MEDITERRANEAN SEA

Betah ●

● Berothai?

● Zobah
a.k.a. Zedad

ARAM

Damascus ●

400 MILES

SEA OF GALILEE

TOB

PHILISTINES

Metheg Ammah?
a.k.a. Gath
●

MOAB

AMALEK   VALLEY OF SALT   EDOM

Map courtesy of The Readable Bible (www.readablebible.com)

— DAY 6 —

Today's Reading: 2 Samuel 8–10

Verse of the Day:

So David reigned over all Israel. And David administered justice and equity to all his people. — 2 Samuel 8:15

Questions for Reflection and Discussion

1. What did David do for Mephibosheth and why?
2. What did Joab say to his brother Abishai as he faced the army of Ammon?

Notes on Today's Bible Reading

_____

_____

_____

_____

_____

_____

_____

_____

_____

_____

_____

_____

_____

_____

— DAY 7 —

Review of This Week's Readings:
1 Samuel 26–31; 2 Samuel 1–10

Questions for Reflection and Discussion

1. What passage uniquely spoke to you this week?

2. What insights did you gain about God?

3. What application might this have to what is happening in the world today?

4. How would God have you apply this truth to your life?

Notes from Reflecting on This Week's Bible Readings

Week 23

How can one sin snowball out of control into a host of others? Find out from David in 2 Samuel.

— DAY 1 —
Today's Reading: 2 Samuel 11–12

Verse of the Day:

It happened, late one afternoon, when David arose from his couch and was walking on the roof of the king's house, that he saw from the roof a woman bathing; and the woman was very beautiful. — 2 Samuel 11:2

Questions for Reflection and Discussion

1. What does chapter 11 suggest David should have been doing that would have kept him from his encounter with Bathsheba?

2. What responsibility did God give to Nathan the prophet?

Notes on Today's Bible Reading

— DAY 2 —

Today's Reading: 2 Samuel 13

Verse of the Day:

But Absalom fled and went to Talmai the son of Ammihud, king of Geshur. And David mourned for his son day after day. — 2 Samuel 13:37

Questions for Reflection and Discussion

1. Did David's actions and behavior influence his children's actions and behavior, or was it only coincidental?

2. How did the events in this chapter relate to Nathan's prophetic word?

Notes on Today's Bible Reading

— DAY 3 —

Today's Reading: 2 Samuel 14

Verse of the Day:

Now in all Israel there was no one so much to be praised for his handsome appearance as Absalom. From the sole of his foot to the crown of his head there was no blemish in him. — 2 Samuel 14:25

Questions for Reflection and Discussion

1. What does this chapter say about Absalom's physical appearance?

2. After David had banished Absalom from his presence for two years, what did the king do when he was finally reunited with his wayward son?

Notes on Today's Bible Reading

— DAY 4 —

Today's Reading: 2 Samuel 15

Verse of the Day:

Then Absalom would say, "Oh that I were judge in the land! Then every man with a dispute or cause might come to me, and I would give him justice." — 2 Samuel 15:4

Questions for Reflection and Discussion

1. How was Absalom able to steal "the hearts of the men of Israel" away from loyalty to David and start a civil war?

2. When the priests carried the ark of the covenant out of Jerusalem and were ordered to return with it, what did David tell them about God and His purposes?

Notes on Today's Bible Reading

— DAY 5 —
Today's Reading: 2 Samuel 16–17

Verse of the Day:

"It may be that the Lord will look on the wrong done to me, and that the Lord will repay me with good for his cursing today." — 2 Samuel 16:12

Questions for Reflection and Discussion

1. When the deposed king and his entourage fled Jerusalem, they encountered the abusive Shimei yet allowed him to live. What was David's desire from the Lord?

2. How did Hushai describe David and his valiant men to Absalom?

Notes on Today's Bible Reading

— DAY 6 —

Today's Reading: 2 Samuel 18

Verse of the Day:

And the king was deeply moved and went up to the chamber over the gate and wept. And as he went, he said, "O my son Absalom, my son, my son Absalom! Would I had died instead of you, O Absalom, my son, my son!" — 2 Samuel 18:33

Questions for Reflection and Discussion

1. What did David command Joab and the other commanders regarding Absalom, and what did Joab do instead?

2. When David heard the good news of decisive victory over the insurrectionist army followed by the bad news about his son's death, how did he respond?

Notes on Today's Bible Reading

— DAY 7 —
Review of This Week's Readings:
2 Samuel 11–18

Questions for Reflection and Discussion

1. What passage uniquely spoke to you this week?
2. What insights did you gain about God?
3. What application might this have to what is happening in the world today?
4. How would God have you apply this truth to your life?

Notes from Reflecting on This Week's Bible Readings

_____

_____

_____

_____

_____

_____

_____

_____

_____

_____

_____

_____

_____

_____

_____

_____

When innocents are suffering, what is one thing everyone can do? Find out from David as we conclude 2 Samuel.

— DAY 1 —
Today's Reading: 2 Samuel 19

Verse of the Day:

"You are my brothers; you are my bone and my flesh. Why then should you be the last to bring back the king?" — 2 Samuel 19:12

Questions for Reflection and Discussion

1. For what strategic purpose did Joab urge King David to suspend his grief over Absalom?

2. What was the basis for the disagreement between the ten tribes of Israel and the tribe of Judah in the aftermath of the king's victory over Absalom's insurrection?

Notes on Today's Bible Reading

— DAY 2 —

Today's Reading: 2 Samuel 20–21

Verse of the Day:

Now there was a famine in the days of David for three years, year after year. And David sought the face of the LORD. — 2 Samuel 21:1a

Questions for Reflection and Discussion

1. What compromise did Joab offer the wise woman during his quest to apprehend the insurrectionist Sheba, who was hiding in her besieged city?

2. In response to the famine that lasted for three years, what was the first thing King David did?

Notes on Today's Bible Reading

_____

_____

_____

_____

_____

_____

_____

_____

_____

_____

_____

_____

_____

— DAY 3 —

Today's Reading: 2 Samuel 22

Verse of the Day:

"In my distress I called upon the Lord;
　　to my God I called.
From his temple he heard my voice,
　　and my cry came to his ears." — 2 Samuel 22:7

Questions for Reflection and Discussion

1. How did God respond when David called to Him in his distress?

2. Why was David's repeated reference to God as his Rock especially relevant during this time?

Notes on Today's Bible Reading

— DAY 4 —

Today's Reading: 2 Samuel 23–24

Verse of the Day:

But the king said to Araunah, "No, but I will buy it from you for a price. I will not offer burnt offerings to the LORD my God that cost me nothing." So David bought the threshing floor and the oxen for fifty shekels of silver. — 2 Samuel 24:24

Questions for Reflection and Discussion

1. After longing for water from a well in Philistine-held territory, why did David refuse to drink when his mighty men brought it to him, and what did he do with the water?

2. When God sent a plague and the prophet Gad gave instruction to build an altar to the Lord at the threshing floor of Araunah, how did David respond when Araunah offered animals for David to sacrifice?

Notes on Today's Bible Reading

For an introduction to 1 Chronicles, see appendix 1, page 394.

— DAY 5 —

Today's Reading: 1 Chronicles 1–2

Verses of the Day:

These are the sons of Israel: Reuben, Simeon, Levi, Judah, Issachar, Zebulun, Dan, Joseph, Benjamin, Naphtali, Gad, and Asher.
— 1 Chronicles 2:1–2

Questions for Reflection and Discussion

1. Who was the first man on earth to be a "mighty man"?
2. What were the names of the twelve sons of Israel?

Notes on Today's Bible Reading

— DAY 6 —

Today's Reading: 1 Chronicles 3–5

Verses of the Day:

Jabez was more honorable than his brothers; and his mother called his name Jabez, saying, "Because I bore him in pain." Jabez called upon the God of Israel, saying, "Oh that you would bless me and enlarge my border, and that your hand might be with me, and that you would keep me from harm so that it might not bring me pain!" And God granted what he asked. — 1 Chronicles 4:9–10

Questions for Reflection and Discussion

1. What did Jabez ask of the Lord, and how did God respond?

2. Why did God hand over the Hagrites and all their allies in battle to the Israeli tribes of Reuben, Gad, and the half-tribe of Manasseh?

Notes on Today's Bible Reading

_____

_____

_____

_____

_____

_____

_____

_____

_____

_____

— DAY 7 —

Review of This Week's Readings:
2 Samuel 19–24; 1 Chronicles 1–5

Questions for Reflection and Discussion

1. What passage uniquely spoke to you this week?

2. What insights did you gain about God?

3. What application might this have to what is happening in the world today?

4. How would God have you apply this truth to your life?

Notes from Reflecting on This Week's Bible Readings

When facing challenges, how can we navigate them? Find out from the men of Issachar in 1 Chronicles this week.

— DAY 1 —
Today's Reading: 1 Chronicles 6

Verse of the Day:

They ministered with song before the tabernacle of the tent of meeting until Solomon built the house of the LORD in Jerusalem, and they performed their service according to their order. — 1 Chronicles 6:32

Questions for Reflection and Discussion

1. Once the ark of God rested at the tent of meeting, what service did David assign the Kohathites?

2. What traditional duties were assigned to Aaron's descendants with respect to the tabernacle?

Notes on Today's Bible Reading

— DAY 2 —

Today's Reading: 1 Chronicles 7–8

Verse of the Day:

The sons of Tola [were] mighty warriors of their generations.
— 1 Chronicles 7:2a

Questions for Reflection and Discussion

1. How were the men of the tribes of Issachar, Benjamin, and Asher characterized?

2. In the genealogy of Saul, what special skill did the sons of Ulam possess?

Notes on Today's Bible Reading

— DAY 3 —

Today's Reading: 1 Chronicles 9–10

Verse of the Day:

And Phinehas the son of Eleazar was the chief officer over them in time past; the LORD was with him. — 1 Chronicles 9:20

Questions for Reflection and Discussion

1. Why were the singers who lodged in the chambers of the temple free of other duties?

2. Scripture tells us Saul died for his "breach of faith," a common theme of Chronicles. Name one of the ways Saul was unfaithful to the Lord.

Notes on Today's Bible Reading

— DAY 4 —

Today's Reading: 1 Chronicles 11–12

Verse of the Day:

Of Issachar, men who had understanding of the times, to know what Israel ought to do, 200 chiefs, and all their kinsmen under their command. — 1 Chronicles 12:32

Questions for Reflection and Discussion

1. How did Joab become chief and commander of David's army?

2. When divisions of armed troops from every tribe in Israel came to David at Hebron to turn the kingdom of Saul over to him, how does Scripture describe the sons of Issachar?

Notes on Today's Bible Reading

— DAY 5 —

Today's Reading: 1 Chronicles 13–15

Verse of the Day:

"Then let us bring again the ark of our God to us, for we did not seek it in the days of Saul." — 1 Chronicles 13:3

Questions for Reflection and Discussion

1. Why was David's first attempt to bring the ark of God to the city of David unsuccessful, resulting in Uzzah's death? What measures did David take to assure a safe return of the ark?

2. When Michal, David's wife, saw him from her window celebrating with music and dancing as the ark entered Jerusalem, how did she react?

Notes on Today's Bible Reading

— DAY 6 —

Today's Reading: 1 Chronicles 16–17

Verse of the Day:

Oh give thanks to the Lord; call upon His name;
> make known his deeds among the peoples! — 1 Chronicles 16:8

Questions for Reflection and Discussion

1. Asaph and his brothers were appointed to give thanks and make music to the Lord continually. Describe David's song of thanksgiving following the return of the ark.

2. What did David desire to do for the Lord? What was God's response through His prophet Nathan?

Notes on Today's Bible Reading

— DAY 7 —
Review of This Week's Readings:
1 Chronicles 6–17

Questions for Reflection and Discussion

1. What passage uniquely spoke to you this week?

2. What insights did you gain about God?

3. What application might this have to what is happening in the world today?

4. How would God have you apply this truth to your life?

Notes from Reflecting on This Week's Bible Readings

In a world full of opposition and strife, how can we find courage and peace? Find out from David as we begin the book of Psalms.

— DAY 1 —

Today's Reading: 1 Chronicles 18–20

Verse of the Day:

Then David put garrisons in Syria of Damascus, and the Syrians became servants to David and brought tribute. And the LORD gave victory to David wherever he went. — 1 Chronicles 18:6

Questions for Reflection and Discussion

1. What did David do with all the riches that King Tou gave him and that he won in battle?

2. Whose crown did David take for himself?

Notes on Today's Bible Reading

— DAY 2 —

Today's Reading: 1 Chronicles 21–23

Verse of the Day:

"Then you will prosper if you are careful to observe the statutes and the rules that the Lord commanded Moses for Israel. Be strong and courageous. Fear not; do not be dismayed." — 1 Chronicles 22:13

Questions for Reflection and Discussion

1. Comparing 1 Chronicles 21 with 2 Samuel 24, who prompted David to number the people? Do the opening chapters of the book of Job help resolve this apparent contradiction?

2. When David commanded all the leaders of Israel to help his son Solomon, what did he encourage them to do in response to God's goodness to the nation?

Notes on Today's Bible Reading

— DAY 3 —

Today's Reading: 1 Chronicles 24–26

Verse of the Day:

But Nadab and Abihu died before their father and had no children,
so Eleazar and Ithamar became the priests. — 1 Chronicles 24:2

Questions for Reflection and Discussion

1. Can you remember why Nadab and Abihu, the sons of Aaron, "died before their father and had no children"? (Hint: Leviticus 10)

2. How was the order for service determined between the various priestly families?

Notes on Today's Bible Reading

— DAY 4 —

Today's Reading: 1 Chronicles 27–29

Verse of the Day:

"Now therefore in the sight of all Israel, the assembly of the LORD, and in the hearing of our God, observe and seek out all the commandments of the LORD your God, that you may possess this good land and leave it for an inheritance to your children after you forever." — 1 Chronicles 28:8

Questions for Reflection and Discussion

1. David told the people of his desire to build a house for God, but why did God not allow him to do so?

2. As David prayed over the offering of all the material to build the temple, where did he say all the gold, silver, wood, precious stones, and other materials came from?

Notes on Today's Bible Reading

— DAY 5 —

Today's Reading: Psalms 1–5

For an introduction to Psalms, see appendix 1, page 396.

Verse of the Day:

Blessed is the man
> who walks not in the counsel of the wicked,
nor stands in the way of sinners,
> nor sits in the seat of scoffers. — Psalm 1:1

Questions for Reflection and Discussion

1. David said many rose up against him to trouble him and discourage him, but he was able to have peace and courage because:
   a. He called upon God (prayed).
   b. The Lord was David's shield.
   c. The Lord sustained David.
   d. The Lord fought David's battle, striking his enemies.
   e. All the above.

2. When David was surrounded, what three things did he confess about God (3:3)?

Notes on Today's Bible Reading

— DAY 6 —

Today's Reading: Psalms 6–10

Verses of the Day:

O Lord, our Lord,
>   how majestic is your name in all the earth!
You have set your glory above the heavens.
>   Out of the mouth of babies and infants,
you have established strength because of your foes,
>   to still the enemy and the avenger. — Psalm 8:1–2

Questions for Reflection and Discussion

1. David made clear that God is not the God of only Israel; He is the God over all the nations, and as such He will do what?
   a. Ask for their help
   b. Excuse their sin
   c. Judge the entire world
   d. None of the above

2. David recognized that the Lord will not ____ those who know the name of the Lord, trust Him, and seek Him.

Notes on Today's Bible Reading

— DAY 7 —

Review of This Week's Readings:
1 Chronicles 18–29; Psalms 1–10

Questions for Reflection and Discussion

1. What passage uniquely spoke to you this week?

2. What insights did you gain about God?

3. What application might this have to what is happening in the world today?

4. How would God have you apply this truth to your life?

Notes from Reflecting on This Week's Bible Readings

Why is it better to place our trust in God rather than the things of this world? Find out as we continue reading Psalms.

— DAY 1 —

Today's Reading: Psalms 11–16

Verse of the Day:

For the LORD is righteous;
he loves righteous deeds;
    the upright shall behold his face. — Psalm 11:7

Questions for Reflection and Discussion

1. In Psalm 14, what did the fool say?

2. In Psalm 15, what are some characteristics David deemed necessary to enter God's presence?

Notes on Today's Bible Reading

— DAY 2 —

Today's Reading: Psalms 17–18

Verses of the Day:

I love you, O Lord, my strength.
The Lord is my rock and my fortress and my deliverer,
    my God, my rock, in whom I take refuge,
      my shield, and the horn of my salvation, my stronghold.
I will call upon the Lord, who is worthy to be praised,
    and I am saved from my enemies. — Psalm 18:1–3

Questions for Reflection and Discussion

1. In David's prayer for vindication in Psalm 17, what did he mean when he asked God to "keep me as the apple of your eye"?

2. In the opening of David's song of praise in Psalm 18, what are some of the images he used to compare God (v. 2)?
   a. Rock
   b. Fortress
   c. Shield
   d. Stronghold
   e. All of the above

Notes on Today's Bible Reading

— DAY 3 —

Today's Reading: Psalms 19–22

Verse of the Day:

Let the words of my mouth and the meditation of my heart
 be acceptable in your sight,
  O LORD, my rock and my redeemer. — Psalm 19:14

Questions for Reflection and Discussion

1. Where can we clearly see evidence for the glory of God according to Psalm 19?

2. Psalm 22 prophetically describes the crucifixion and resurrection of Christ. Can you identify the direct quote of Jesus to the Father (Matt. 27:46 and Mark 15:34)?

Notes on Today's Bible Reading

_____

_____

_____

_____

_____

_____

_____

_____

_____

_____

_____

_____

— DAY 4 —

Today's Reading: Psalms 23–27

Verse of the Day:

Wait for the LORD;
>   be strong, and let your heart take courage;
>   wait for the LORD! — Psalm 27:14

Questions for Reflection and Discussion

1. In Psalm 24, whose return to Jerusalem is predicted?

2. In Psalm 27, what was the one thing David asked of the Lord and sought after?

Notes on Today's Bible Reading

— DAY 5 —

Today's Reading: Psalms 28–31

Verse of the Day:

The Lord sits enthroned over the flood;
  the Lord sits enthroned as king forever. — Psalm 29:10

Questions for Reflection and Discussion

1. Which of the following describe the voice of the Lord in Psalm 29?
   a. Powerful
   b. Majestic
   c. Breaking
   d. Shaking
   e. All of the above

2. How did God come to David's defense when he was in distress and remembered God's abundant goodness to those who fear the Lord (Psalm 31)?

Notes on Today's Bible Reading

— DAY 6 —

Today's Reading: Psalms 32–34

Verse of the Day:

Oh, taste and see that the LORD is good!

Blessed is the man who takes refuge in him! — Psalm 34:8

Questions for Reflection and Discussion

1. According to David in Psalm 32, who was blessed, and what steps did he take to experience that blessing personally?

2. In Psalm 34, whom did the angel of the Lord encamp around, and what did he do for them?

Notes on Today's Bible Reading

— DAY 7 —
Review of This Week's Readings:
Psalms 11–34

Questions for Reflection and Discussion

1. What passage uniquely spoke to you this week?

2. What insights did you gain about God?

3. What application might this have to what is happening in the world today?

4. How would God have you apply this truth to your life?

Notes from Reflecting on This Week's Bible Readings

What assurance from the Lord do the brokenhearted have? Find out as we continue in the book of Psalms.

— DAY 1 —

Today's Reading: Psalms 35–36

Verses of the Day:

How precious is your steadfast love, O God!
　　The children of mankind take refuge in the shadow
　　of your wings. . . .
For with you is the fountain of life;
　　in your light do we see light. — Psalm 36:7, 9

Questions for Reflection and Discussion

1. What posture of prayer did David adopt in Psalm 35, and what did it indicate about him?

2. What verse in Psalm 36 was quoted by Paul in Romans 3:18 to describe our sinfulness?

Notes on Today's Bible Reading

— DAY 2 —

Today's Reading: Psalm 37

Verses of the Day:

Fret not yourself because of evildoers;
   be not envious of wrongdoers!
For they will soon fade like the grass,
   and wither like the green herb. — Psalm 37:1–2

Questions for Reflection and Discussion

1. If we delight ourselves in the Lord, what does He promise us?

2. Which verse in this psalm provides the foundation for the third Beatitude (Matt. 5:5)?

Notes on Today's Bible Reading

— DAY 3 —

Today's Reading: Psalms 38–41

Verse of the Day:

Blessed is the man who makes
the Lord his trust,
who does not turn to the proud,
to those who go astray after a lie! — Psalm 40:4

Questions for Reflection and Discussion

1. How did David describe the impact of sin on his life in Psalm 38?

2. What prophesy of Jesus's betrayal did you find in Psalm 41? (Hint: John 13:18)

Notes on Today's Bible Reading

— DAY 4 —

Today's Reading: Psalms 42–44

Verse of the Day:

Send out your light and your truth;
    let them lead me;
let them bring me to your holy hill
    and to your dwelling! — Psalm 43:3

Questions for Reflection and Discussion

1. To what did the psalmist compare his desire for the Lord in Psalm 42?

2. What could the nation of Israel place their trust in to achieve victory over their enemies?
    a. Their swords
    b. Their bows
    c. Their strength
    d. God's providential intervention

Notes on Today's Bible Reading

— DAY 5 —

Today's Reading: Psalms 45–48

Verse of the Day:

"Be still, and know that I am God.
  I will be exalted among the nations,
  I will be exalted in the earth!" — Psalm 46:10

Questions for Reflection and Discussion

1. Which verses from Psalm 45 did the writer of Hebrews quote (1:8–9) and apply to Christ?

2. What famous song written by Reformer Martin Luther is based on Psalm 46?
    a. "Mighty God"
    b. "What a Mighty God We Serve"
    c. "A Mighty Fortress Is Our God"
    d. "Great and Mighty Is the Lord Our God"

Notes on Today's Bible Reading

— DAY 6 —

Today's Reading: Psalms 49–50

Verse of the Day:

Our God comes; he does not keep silence;
    before him is a devouring fire,
    around him a mighty tempest. — Psalm 50:3

Questions for Reflection and Discussion

1. According to Psalm 49, what certainty do we all face, whether rich or poor, great or small? (Hint: Heb. 9:27)

2. According to Psalm 50, what sacrifice does God desire more than the offering of animals?

Notes on Today's Bible Reading

— DAY 7 —
Review of This Week's Readings:
Psalms 35–50

Questions for Reflection and Discussion

1. What passage uniquely spoke to you this week?

2. What insights did you gain about God?

3. What application might this have to what is happening in the world today?

4. How would God have you apply this truth to your life?

Notes from Reflecting on This Week's Bible Readings

Week 29

Why is God especially worthy of our praise? Find out from David as we continue the book of Psalms.

— DAY 1 —

Today's Reading: Psalms 51–54

Verse of the Day:

Create in me a clean heart, O God,
    and renew a right spirit within me. — Psalm 51:10

Questions for Reflection and Discussion

1. Against whom did David say he sinned in Psalm 51, which was written after the prophet Nathan confronted him (2 Samuel 11–12)?
    a. Bathsheba because of seduction and adultery
    b. Uriah because of adultery and murder
    c. Joab because of David's order making him an accessory to murder
    d. Israel because of deception and hypocrisy
    e. God

2. In Paul's indictment of our utter sinfulness in Romans 3 (especially vv. 11–12), what verses did he quote from Psalm 53?

Notes on Today's Bible Reading

— DAY 2 —

Today's Reading: Psalms 55–57

Verse of the Day:

Cast your burden on the LORD,
    and he will sustain you;
he will never permit
    the righteous to be moved. — Psalm 55:22

Questions for Reflection and Discussion

1. In Psalm 55, what did David say he wished he had to escape his troubles?

2. In Psalm 56, how did David describe God's intimate knowledge and record of his personal struggles?

Notes on Today's Bible Reading

— DAY 3 —
Today's Reading: Psalms 58–61

Verses of the Day:

Oh, grant us help against the foe,
    for vain is the salvation of man!
With God we shall do valiantly;
    it is he who will tread down our foes. — Psalm 60:11–12

Questions for Reflection and Discussion

1. According to Psalm 58, when do the wicked begin to go astray and speak lies?

2. In Psalm 61, where did David ask God to lead him when his heart became faint?

Notes on Today's Bible Reading

_____

_____

_____

_____

_____

_____

_____

_____

_____

_____

_____

_____

_____

— DAY 4 —

Today's Reading: Psalms 62–65

Verses of the Day:

For God alone, O my soul, wait in silence,
    for my hope is from him.
He only is my rock and my salvation,
    my fortress; I shall not be shaken. — Psalm 62:5–6

Questions for Reflection and Discussion

1. Based on Psalm 64, what comes of evildoers?

2. Identify a reason for David's worship of God from Psalm 65:
    a. He hears our prayers.
    b. He atones for our transgressions.
    c. He establishes mountains and stills stormy seas.
    d. He waters the earth and brings forth abundance.
    e. All of the above.

Notes on Today's Bible Reading

— DAY 5 —

Today's Reading: Psalms 66–68

Verse of the Day:

Come and see what God has done:
> he is awesome in his deeds toward the children of man.
> — Psalm 66:5

Questions for Reflection and Discussion

1. What period in Israel's history is reflected in Psalm 66?

2. In the majestic words of Psalm 68, there is a reference in verse 18 Paul picked up in Ephesians 4:8; but for him, who were the captives, and what were these gifts?

Notes on Today's Bible Reading

— DAY 6 —

Today's Reading: Psalms 69–70

Verse of the Day:

May all who seek you
    rejoice and be glad in you!
May those who love your salvation
    say evermore, "God is great!" — Psalm 70:4

Questions for Reflection and Discussion

1. What verse from Psalm 69 is quoted by John's Gospel in reference to Jesus cleansing the temple? (Hint: John 2:17)

2. What expression did David's enemies make in Psalm 70:3, and what expression should God's people make according to verse 4?

Notes on Today's Bible Reading

— DAY 7 —
Review of This Week's Readings:
Psalms 51–70

Questions for Reflection and Discussion

1. What passage uniquely spoke to you this week?
2. What insights did you gain about God?
3. What application might this have to what is happening in the world today?
4. How would God have you apply this truth to your life?

Notes from Reflecting on This Week's Bible Readings

What will happen to the wicked who seem to be winning? Find out as we continue studying the book of Psalms.

— DAY 1 —

Today's Reading: Psalms 71–72

Verse of the Day:

Be to me a rock of refuge,
    to which I may continually come;
you have given the command to save me,
    for you are my rock and my fortress. — Psalm 71:3

Questions for Reflection and Discussion

1. What is the general age of the anonymous psalmist who wrote Psalm 71?
   a. A young boy?
   b. An elderly adult?
   c. A young adult?
   d. A man in his prime?

2. In one of only two psalms Solomon wrote, Psalm 72 focuses on the coronation of the king, but its words found ultimate fulfillment in whom?

Notes on Today's Bible Reading

— DAY 2 —

Today's Reading: Psalms 73–74

Verse of the Day:

My flesh and my heart may fail;
> but God is the strength of my heart and my portion
> forever. — Psalm 73:26

Questions for Reflection and Discussion

1. In Psalm 73, Asaph asked the age-old question, Why do the wicked prosper? However, what evidence is there that Asaph came to his senses about God's justice?

2. In Psalm 74, Asaph seemed to think God rejected His people because of the bad circumstances they experienced. When are you more likely to think God may be rejecting you?

Notes on Today's Bible Reading

— DAY 3 —

Today's Reading: Psalms 75–77

Verse of the Day:

For not from the east or from the west
  and not from the wilderness comes lifting up,
but it is God who executes judgment,
  putting down one and lifting up another. — Psalm 75:6–7

Questions for Reflection and Discussion

1. What attribute of God is on display in Psalm 75?
   a. Mercy
   b. Grace
   c. Justice
   d. None of the above

2. In Psalm 77, Asaph seemed to be losing hope, but what did he do that changed his perspective?

Notes on Today's Bible Reading

— DAY 4 —

Today's Reading: Psalm 78

Verse of the Day:

We will not hide them from their children,
    but tell to the coming generation
the glorious deeds of the LORD, and his might,
    and the wonders that he has done. — Psalm 78:4

Questions for Reflection and Discussion

1. According to Asaph, what can we do to help ensure future generations do not follow in the footsteps and failures of those who preceded them?

2. After walking us through the history of Israel to that point, Asaph concluded this psalm with what two descriptions of King David's leadership (v. 72)?

Notes on Today's Bible Reading

— DAY 5 —

Today's Reading: Psalms 79–81

Verse of the Day:

"But we your people, the sheep of your pasture,
      will give thanks to you forever;
      from generation to generation we will recount
   your praise." — Psalm 79:13

Questions for Reflection and Discussion

1. In Psalm 79, what did Asaph report that apparently happened to Jerusalem and the temple?

2. In Psalm 81, what did the Lord promise to His people if only they would listen to Him and walk in His ways (vv. 13–14)?

Notes on Today's Bible Reading

— DAY 6 —

Today's Reading: Psalms 82–85

Verse of the Day:

For a day in your courts is better
     than a thousand elsewhere.
I would rather be a doorkeeper in the house of my God
     than dwell in the tents of wickedness. — Psalm 84:10

Questions for Reflection and Discussion

1. In Psalm 82, to what is the psalmist referring in the phrase, "You are gods, sons of the Most High"? (Hint: John 10:34–39)
   a. The word *gods* refers to angelic beings.
   b. The word *gods* refers to pagan deities.
   c. The word *gods* refers to human authorities, who in a sense stand in the place of God in their ability to determine the fate of others.
   d. None of the above.

2. What job in the house of God did the psalmist say in Psalm 84 he would rather have than "dwell in the tents of wickedness"?

Notes on Today's Bible Reading

_____

_____

_____

_____

_____

_____

_____

_____

— DAY 7 —
Review of This Week's Readings:
Psalms 71–85

Questions for Reflection and Discussion

1. What passage uniquely spoke to you this week?

2. What insights did you gain about God?

3. What application might this have to what is happening in the world today?

4. How would God have you apply this truth to your life?

Notes from Reflecting on This Week's Bible Readings

What are the benefits of walking with integrity before the Lord? Find out as we continue the book of Psalms.

— DAY 1 —

Today's Reading: Psalms 86–88

Verse of the Day:

All the nations you have made shall come
and worship before you, O Lord,
and shall glorify your name. — Psalm 86:9

Questions for Reflection and Discussion

1. Can you identify a characteristic of God mentioned in Psalm 86?
   a. Good
   b. Forgiving
   c. Merciful
   d. All of the above

2. What does the Lord record as He "registers the peoples" in Psalm 87?

Notes on Today's Bible Reading

_____

_____

_____

_____

_____

_____

_____

_____

_____

— DAY 2 —
Today's Reading: Psalm 89

Verses of the Day:

Righteousness and justice are the foundation of your throne;
    steadfast love and faithfulness go before you.
Blessed are the people who know the festal shout,
    who walk, O Lord, in the light of your face. — Psalm 89:14–15

Questions for Reflection and Discussion

1. Of the mighty acts of God mentioned in Psalm 89, which one did Jesus perform in the presence of His fearful disciples? (Hint: Matt. 8:23–27)

2. What two virtues did the psalmist describe as the foundation of God's throne?

Notes on Today's Bible Reading

— DAY 3 —

Today's Reading: Psalms 90–93

Verses of the Day:

So teach us to number our days
    that we may get a heart of wisdom. . . .
Let the favor of the Lord our God be upon us,
    and establish the work of our hands upon us;
    yes, establish the work of our hands! — Psalm 90:12, 17

Questions for Reflection and Discussion

1. In Psalm 90, Moses lamented the brevity of life. Which of the following requests did he not make of God?
    a. Grant us long life
    b. Satisfy us with Your love so that we may rejoice and be glad
    c. Let Your favor be upon us
    d. Establish the work of our hands

2. In Psalm 91, God made a number of wonderful promises regarding health and safety, but to whom do these promises apply?

Notes on Today's Bible Reading

— DAY 4 —

Today's Reading: Psalms 96–97

Verse of the Day:

O you who love the LORD, hate evil!
> He preserves the lives of his saints;
> he delivers them from the hand of the wicked. — Psalm 97:10

Questions for Reflection and Discussion

1. According to Psalm 94, what is God's expectation regarding evildoers (v. 16)?

2. According to Psalm 95, when we hear God's voice, what must we never do?

Notes on Today's Bible Reading

— DAY 5 —

Today's Reading: Psalms 98–102

Verse of the Day:

For the LORD is good;
> his steadfast love endures forever,
> and his faithfulness to all generations. — Psalm 100:5

Questions for Reflection and Discussion

1. According to Psalm 100, with what are we to enter God's gates?

2. In Psalm 101, the psalmist said he would not set before his eyes anything that is
_____.

Notes on Today's Bible Reading

— DAY 6 —

Today's Reading: Psalms 103–4

Verses of the Day:

But the steadfast love of the LORD is from everlasting to everlasting
on those who fear him,
    and his righteousness to children's children,
to those who keep his covenant
    and remember to do his commandments. — Psalm 103:17–18

Questions for Reflection and Discussion

1. When the psalmist said that God "made known his ways to Moses, [but] his acts to the people of Israel" (103:7), what is the difference?

2. What animals are found in Psalm 104?
   a. Wild goats
   b. Rock badgers
   c. Lions
   d. Leviathan
   e. All the above

Notes on Today's Bible Reading

— DAY 7 —
Review of This Week's Readings:
Psalms 86–104

Questions for Reflection and Discussion

1. What passage uniquely spoke to you this week?

2. What insights did you gain about God?

3. What application might this have to what is happening in the world today?

4. How would God have you apply this truth to your life?

Notes from Reflecting on This Week's Bible Readings

_____

_____

_____

_____

_____

_____

_____

_____

_____

_____

_____

_____

_____

_____

Why is it good to fear the Lord? Find out as we continue reading the book of Psalms this week.

— DAY 1 —

Today's Reading: Psalm 105

Verses of the Day:

Oh give thanks to the LORD; call upon his name;
    make known his deeds among the peoples!
Sing to him, sing psalms to him;
    tell of all his wondrous works! — Psalm 105:1–2

Questions for Reflection and Discussion

1. What did God say by way of rebuke to kings regarding the patriarchs (v. 15)?
2. What were the practical functions of the cloud by day and of fire by night (v. 39)?

Notes on Today's Bible Reading

— DAY 2 —
Today's Reading: Psalm 106

Verse of the Day:

But they soon forgot his works;
    they did not wait for his counsel. — Psalm 106:13

Questions for Reflection and Discussion

1. Who intervened when Israel succumbed to idolatry, and it was credited to him for righteousness (vv. 30–31)?

2. When Israel served idols, to whom were they really sacrificing their sons and daughters according to the psalmist (vv. 36–37)?

Notes on Today's Bible Reading

— DAY 3 —
Today's Reading: Psalm 107

Verse of the Day:

Then they cried to the LORD in their trouble,
and he delivered them from their distress. — Psalm 107:28

Questions for Reflection and Discussion

1. What is the reason the psalmist called upon people to give thanks to the Lord?

2. What do you think the psalmist meant by God "sent out his word and healed them, and delivered them from their destruction"?

Notes on Today's Bible Reading

— DAY 4 —

Today's Reading: Psalms 108–10

Verses of the Day:

Help me, O LORD my God!
> Save me according to your steadfast love!
Let them know that this is your hand;
> you, O LORD, have done it! — Psalm 109:26–27

Questions for Reflection and Discussion

1. How did David say he would "do valiantly"?
   a. Good preparation
   b. An overwhelming force of men
   c. Through God
   d. All of the above

2. In Psalm 109, David asked the Lord to deal with him based upon what?

Notes on Today's Bible Reading

— DAY 5 —

Today's Reading: Psalms 111–15

Verse of the Day:

Great are the works of the LORD,
> studied by all who delight in them. — Psalm 111:2

Questions for Reflection and Discussion

1. According to Psalm 111, the works of the Lord are pondered by all who delight in them. Which works did the psalmist note?
    a. He provides food for those who fear him.
    b. He gave them the inheritance of the nations.
    c. He sent redemption to His people.
    d. All of the above.

2. According to Psalm 112, what does God promise to the upright when they find themselves in a dark place in life? (Hint: v. 4)

Notes on Today's Bible Reading

— DAY 6 —

Today's Reading: Psalms 116–18

Verse of the Day:

I will offer to you the sacrifice of thanksgiving
and call on the name of the LORD. — Psalm 116:17

Questions for Reflection and Discussion

1. In Psalm 116, how did the psalmist describe the death of the saints?

2. What future event did the psalmist depict in Psalm 118:26 and following? (Hint: Luke 19:38)

Notes on Today's Bible Reading

— DAY 7 —
Review of This Week's Readings:
Psalms 105–18

Questions for Reflection and Discussion

1. What passage uniquely spoke to you this week?

2. What insights did you gain about God?

3. What application might this have to what is happening in the world today?

4. How would God have you apply this truth to your life?

Notes from Reflecting on This Week's Bible Readings

What can we do to help keep us from sinning? Find out this week as we continue the book of Psalms.

— DAY 1 —

Today's Reading: Psalm 119:1–48

Verse of the Day:

Open my eyes, that I may behold
   wondrous things out of your law. — Psalm 119:18

Questions for Reflection and Discussion

1. According to Psalm 119:9–16, how can young people keep their way pure?

2. What was the psalmist's attitude toward God's law?
   a. Disdain
   b. Disregard
   c. Delight
   d. None of the above

Notes on Today's Bible Reading

— DAY 2 —

Today's Reading: Psalm 119:49–96

Verse of the Day:

The law of your mouth is better to me
      than thousands of gold and silver pieces. — Psalm 119:72

Questions for Reflection and Discussion

1. What was it that gave the Lord's servant hope and comfort in affliction according to Psalm 119:49–50?

2. Why did the psalmist say, "It is good for me that I was afflicted" (v. 71)?

Notes on Today's Bible Reading

— DAY 3 —

Today's Reading: Psalm 119:97–144

Verse of the Day:

Your word is a lamp to my feet
     and a light to my path. — Psalm 119:105

Questions for Reflection and Discussion

1. Speaking of God's word, the psalmist declared, "Your word is a _____ to my feet and a _____ to my path."

2. In verse 126, what reason did the psalmist give for declaring that it was time for the Lord to act?

Notes on Today's Bible Reading

_____

_____

_____

_____

_____

_____

_____

_____

_____

_____

_____

_____

_____

— DAY 4 —

Today's Reading: Psalm 119:145–76

Verse of the Day:

But you are near, O Lord,
  and all your commandments are true. — Psalm 119:151

Questions for Reflection and Discussion

1. According to verse 165, what do those who love God's word possess?

2. When the psalmist confessed, "I have gone astray like a lost sheep," what does he ask the Lord to do? (Hint: v. 176)

Notes on Today's Bible Reading

— DAY 5 —

Today's Reading: Psalms 120–28

Verses of the Day:

Behold, children are a heritage from the Lord,
    the fruit of the womb a reward.
Like arrows in the hand of a warrior
    are the children of one's youth.
Blessed is the man
    who fills his quiver with them!
He shall not be put to shame. — Psalm 127:3–5

Questions for Reflection and Discussion

1. From Psalm 122, what are we instructed to pray concerning Jerusalem?

2. In Psalm 127, how does the psalmist describe children?
    a. They are a blessing.
    b. They are a reward.
    c. They are a heritage from the Lord.
    d. They are like arrows in the hands of a warrior.
    e. All of the above.

Notes on Today's Bible Reading

— DAY 6 —
Today's Reading: Psalms 129–34

Verse of the Day:

Behold, how good and pleasant it is
    when brothers dwell in unity! — Psalm 133:1

Questions for Reflection and Discussion

1. In Psalm 130, the psalmist asked, "If you, O Lord, should mark iniquities, O Lord, who could stand? But with you there is _____." (Hint: v. 4a)

2. According to Psalm 133, what happens when God's people dwell together in unity?

Notes on Today's Bible Reading

— DAY 7 —
Review of This Week's Readings:
Psalms 119–34

Questions for Reflection and Discussion

1. What passage uniquely spoke to you this week?

2. What insights did you gain about God?

3. What application might this have to what is happening in the world today?

4. How would God have you apply this truth to your life?

Notes from Reflecting on This Week's Bible Readings

Week 34

What does God's Word say about life in the womb? Find out as we continue reading through Psalms.

— DAY 1 —

Today's Reading: Psalms 135–37

Verse of the Day:

Whatever the LORD pleases, he does,
    in heaven and on earth,
        in the seas and all deeps. — Psalm 135:6

Questions for Reflection and Discussion

1. What does Psalm 135:15–18 say about those who create idols and those who trust in them?

2. What caused the Israelites to weep in Psalm 137?

Notes on Today's Bible Reading

— DAY 2 —
Today's Reading: Psalms 138–40

Verse of the Day:

I praise you, for I am fearfully and wonderfully made.
Wonderful are your works;
    my soul knows it very well. — Psalm 139:14

Questions for Reflection and Discussion

1. From Psalm 138:2, what had the Lord exalted above all things?

2. The psalmist declared in Psalm 139:13–14a, "You formed my inward parts; you knitted me together in my mother's womb. . . . I am _____ and _____ made."

Notes on Today's Bible Reading

_____

_____

_____

_____

_____

_____

_____

_____

_____

_____

_____

— DAY 3 —

Today's Reading: Psalms 141–44

Verse of the Day:

Let me hear in the morning of your steadfast love,
   for in you I trust.
Make me know the way I should go,
   for to you I lift up my soul. — Psalm 143:8

Questions for Reflection and Discussion

1. What did David ask God to set a guard over?

2. What people did David say are happy?

Notes on Today's Bible Reading

— DAY 4 —

Today's Reading: Psalms 145–50

Verse of the Day:

Blessed is he whose help is the God of Jacob,
    whose hope is in the LORD his God. — Psalm 146:5

Questions for Reflection and Discussion

1. The Lord takes pleasure in _____.
    a. The legs of man
    b. The strength of horses
    c. Those who fear Him
    d. None of the above

2. In Psalm 148, who and/or what did the psalmist say should praise the Lord?

Notes on Today's Bible Reading

For an introduction
to 1 Kings,
see appendix 1,
page 397.

— DAY 5 —

Today's Reading: 1 Kings 1

Verse of the Day:

"As the LORD has been with my lord the king, even so may he be
with Solomon, and make his throne greater than the throne of my
lord King David." — 1 Kings 1:37

Questions for Reflection and Discussion

1. What did King David fail to do that doubtless contributed to the delinquency of his
son Adonijah (v. 6)?
    a. Give him an allowance
    b. Play catch with him
    c. Discipline and correct him
    d. None of the above

2. After Adonijah's failed attempt to seize his father's throne, newly crowned King Solomon gave him a reprieve on what condition (v. 52)?

Notes on Today's Bible Reading

— DAY 6 —

Today's Reading: 1 Kings 2

Verses of the Day:

"I am about to go the way of all the earth. Be strong, and show yourself a man, and keep the charge of the LORD your God, walking in his ways and keeping his statutes, his commandments, his rules, and his testimonies, as it is written in the Law of Moses, that you may prosper in all that you do and wherever you turn." — 1 Kings 2:2–3

Questions for Reflection and Discussion

1. As Solomon began his tenure as the new king of Israel, what final requests did his father, David, make?
   a. Keep the charge of the Lord, walking in His ways and keeping His commands
   b. Don't let Joab, who is guilty of much bloodshed, die in peace
   c. Take out Shimei, who cursed David when he was fleeing Absalom
   d. All of the above

2. How did King Solomon respond to his brother Adonijah's impudent request?

Notes on Today's Bible Reading

— DAY 7 —
Review of This Week's Readings:
Psalms 135–50; 1 Kings 1–2

Questions for Reflection and Discussion

1. What passage uniquely spoke to you this week?

2. What insights did you gain about God?

3. What application might this have to what is happening in the world today?

4. How would God have you apply this truth to your life?

Notes from Reflecting on This Week's Bible Readings

How can we get wisdom? Find out as we begin the book of Proverbs this week.

For an introduction to Proverbs, see appendix 1, page 398.

— DAY 1 —

Today's Reading: Proverbs 1–2

Verse of the Day:

The fear of the LORD is the beginning of knowledge;
 fools despise wisdom and instruction. — Proverbs 1:7

Questions for Reflection and Discussion

1. According to Solomon in Proverbs 1, what is the fear of the Lord?

2. To better understand the fear of the Lord, what are some things we can do according to Proverbs 2?
    a. Make our ear attentive and heart open to wisdom and understanding
    b. Call out to God for insight and understanding
    c. Seek wisdom like searching for hidden treasures
    d. All of the above

Notes on Today's Bible Reading

— DAY 2 —

Today's Reading: Proverbs 3–4

Verses of the Day:

Trust in the LORD with all your heart,
    and do not lean on your own understanding.
In all your ways acknowledge him,
    and he will make straight your paths. — Proverbs 3:5–6

Questions for Reflection and Discussion

1. According to Proverbs 3:5–6, what is required to make us eligible for God's clear direction for our lives?
    a. Skepticism
    b. Self-reliance
    c. Self-promotion
    d. None of the above

2. According to Proverbs 4:23, why should we be diligent about guarding our hearts?

Notes on Today's Bible Reading

— DAY 3 —

Today's Reading: Proverbs 5–6

Verses of the Day:

Let your fountain be blessed,
>   and rejoice in the wife of your youth,
>   a lovely deer, a graceful doe.
Let her breasts fill you at all times with delight;
>   be intoxicated always in her love. — Proverbs 5:18–19

Questions for Reflection and Discussion

1. How can we avoid the destructive sin explained in Proverbs 5?

2. What are some of the things the Lord hates according to Proverbs 6?
   a. Pride
   b. Deception
   c. Murder
   d. Discord
   e. All of the above

Notes on Today's Bible Reading

_____

_____

_____

_____

_____

_____

_____

_____

_____

_____

— DAY 4 —

Today's Reading: Proverbs 7–8

Verses of the Day:

My son, keep my words
    and treasure up my commandments with you;
keep my commandments and live;
    keep my teaching as the apple of your eye. — Proverbs 7:1–2

Questions for Reflection and Discussion

1. What is the danger to avoid in Proverbs 7?

2. In Proverbs 8, the fear of the Lord is equated with the hatred of _____.

Notes on Today's Bible Reading

— DAY 5 —

Today's Reading: Proverbs 9–10

Verses of the Day:

Whoever winks the eye causes trouble,
    and a babbling fool will come to ruin.
The mouth of the righteous is a fountain of life,
    but the mouth of the wicked conceals violence. — Proverbs 10:10–11

Questions for Reflection and Discussion

1. Which "lady" should a man heed in Proverbs 9?

2. According to Proverbs 10:12, hatred stirs up strife, but what does love do?

Notes on Today's Bible Reading

— DAY 6 —

Today's Reading: Proverbs 11–12

Verse of the Day:

With his mouth the godless man would destroy his neighbor,
    but by knowledge the righteous are delivered. — Proverbs 11:9

Questions for Reflection and Discussion

1. In Proverbs 11, what is like a gold ring in a pig's snout?

2. According to Proverbs 12, an excellent wife is like a _____ for her husband.

Notes on Today's Bible Reading

— DAY 7 —
Review of This Week's Readings:
Proverbs 1–12

Questions for Reflection and Discussion

1. What passage uniquely spoke to you this week?

2. What insights did you gain about God?

3. What application might this have to what is happening in the world today?

4. How would God have you apply this truth to your life?

Notes from Reflecting on This Week's Bible Readings

What does the Lord promise if we commit our work to Him? Find out this week as we continue studying the book of Proverbs.

— DAY 1 —

Today's Reading: Proverbs 13–14

Verse of the Day:

The teaching of the wise is a fountain of life,
　　　that one may turn away from the snares of death. — Proverbs 13:14

Questions for Reflection and Discussion

1. In Proverbs 13, "Whoever spares the rod _____ his son, but he who _____ him is diligent to discipline him."

2. According to Proverbs 14, the way that seems right can lead to _____.

Notes on Today's Bible Reading

— DAY 2 —

Today's Reading: Proverbs 15–16

Verse of the Day:

Better is a little with the fear of the LORD
than great treasure and trouble with it. — Proverbs 15:16

Questions for Reflection and Discussion

1. In Proverbs 15, what can turn away wrath?
   a. A bribe
   b. A big stick
   c. A soft answer
   d. None of the above

2. According to Proverbs 16, what condition makes it possible for God to cause even our enemies to be at peace with us?

Notes on Today's Bible Reading

— DAY 3 —

Today's Reading: Proverbs 17–18

Verse of the Day:

The name of the LORD is a strong tower;
  the righteous man runs into it and is safe. — Proverbs 18:10

Questions for Reflection and Discussion

1. According to Proverbs 17, when does a real friend love us?
   a. During easy times
   b. During tough times
   c. During happy times
   d. During sad times
   e. All of the above

2. In Proverbs 18, what is a strong tower and place of safety for the righteous?

Notes on Today's Bible Reading

— DAY 4 —

Today's Reading: Proverbs 19–20

Verse of the Day:

The fear of the LORD leads to life,
    and whoever has it rests satisfied;
    he will not be visited by harm. — Proverbs 19:23

Questions for Reflection and Discussion

1. In Proverbs 19:21, whose plans are sure to succeed and stand?

2. According to Proverbs 20, if you love sleep, it will likely result in what?
   a. Sweet dreams
   b. Being rested
   c. Poverty
   d. None of the above

Notes on Today's Bible Reading

— DAY 5 —

Today's Reading: Proverbs 21–22

Verse of the Day:

The king's heart is a stream of water in the hand of the Lord;
he turns it wherever he will. — Proverbs 21:1

Questions for Reflection and Discussion

1. In Proverbs 21, who turns the king's heart wherever he wishes?

2. According to Proverbs 22, what should be chosen rather than great riches?

Notes on Today's Bible Reading

— DAY 6 —

Today's Reading: Proverbs 23

Verse of the Day:

Let not your heart envy sinners,
    but continue in the fear of the Lord all the day.
    — Proverbs 23:17

Questions for Reflection and Discussion

1. In Proverbs 23:4–5, what often happens to desired wealth?

2. According to Proverbs 23:10, what should we not do to ancient landmarks?
    a. Spray paint them
    b. Remove them
    c. Update them
    d. None of the above

Notes on Today's Bible Reading

— DAY 7 —
Review of This Week's Readings:
Proverbs 13–23

Questions for Reflection and Discussion

1. What passage uniquely spoke to you this week?

2. What insights did you gain about God?

3. What application might this have to what is happening in the world today?

4. How would God have you apply this truth to your life?

Notes from Reflecting on This Week's Bible Readings

What are the benefits of walking in wisdom? Find out as we finish the book of Proverbs this week.

— DAY 1 —

Today's Reading: Proverbs 24

Verse of the Day:

By wisdom a house is built,
　　and by understanding it is established. — Proverbs 24:3

Questions for Reflection and Discussion

1. According to Proverbs 24:11–12, who are we to rescue, and what is the result if we do not?

2. At the end of Proverbs 24, the writer recorded his observations about a man's neglected property. What was his conclusion?
　　a. Hard work is a waste of time.
　　b. Hiring out all of the work is the way to go.
　　c. Personal diligence is essential to success.
　　d. None of the above.

Notes on Today's Bible Reading

_____

_____

_____

_____

_____

_____

_____

_____

— DAY 2 —

Today's Reading: Proverbs 25–26

Verse of the Day:

A word fitly spoken
    is like apples of gold in a setting of silver. — Proverbs 25:11

Questions for Reflection and Discussion

1. According to Proverbs 25, how are we to treat our enemies, and what is the result?

2. In Proverbs 26, the writer spends a couple of verses comparing the strife caused by gossip and quarreling to what?
    a. Fire fed by kindling
    b. Water poured from a pitcher
    c. Lava erupting from a volcano
    d. All of the above

Notes on Today's Bible Reading

— DAY 3 —

Today's Reading: Proverbs 27

Verse of the Day:

Iron sharpens iron,
      and one man sharpens another. — Proverbs 27:17

Questions for Reflection and Discussion

1. How did the writer of Proverbs contrast the actions of true and fake friends who were in fact enemies in 27:6?

2. What do you think it means for men to "sharpen" one another (27:17)?

Notes on Today's Bible Reading

— DAY 4 —

Today's Reading: Proverbs 28–29

Verse of the Day:

The fear of man lays a snare,
    but whoever trusts in the LORD is safe. — Proverbs 29:25

Questions for Reflection and Discussion

1. In Proverbs 28, the wicked flee when no one pursues, but the righteous are described as _____.
    a. Wise as a serpent
    b. Harmless as a dove
    c. Bold as a lion
    d. None of the above

2. What is the result when righteous people are in authority and the result when the wicked rule?

Notes on Today's Bible Reading

_____

_____

_____

_____

_____

_____

_____

_____

_____

_____

_____

— DAY 5 —

Today's Reading: Proverbs 30

Verse of the Day:

Every word of God proves true;

      he is a shield to those who take refuge in him. — Proverbs 30:5

Questions for Reflection and Discussion

1. What is the obvious answer to the questions in verse 4? Who did the writer have in mind?

2. What are the two pitfalls of riches or poverty?
   a. Denying the Lord or stealing and thus profaning the name of the Lord
   b. Higher taxes or relying on handouts
   c. Stinginess or covetousness
   d. None of the above

Notes on Today's Bible Reading

— DAY 6 —

Today's Reading: Proverbs 31

Verse of the Day:

Charm is deceitful, and beauty is vain,
      but a woman who fears the LORD is to be praised. — Proverbs 31:30

Questions for Reflection and Discussion

1. The husband of an excellent wife trusts her because she does what (v. 12)?
2. Why is this "Proverbs 31 Woman" worth more than precious jewels?
   a. She is an entrepreneur.
   b. She is physically fit.
   c. She is a wise teacher.
   d. She fears the Lord.
   e. All of the above.

Notes on Today's Bible Reading

— DAY 7 —
Review of This Week's Readings:
Proverbs 24–31

Questions for Reflection and Discussion

1. What passage uniquely spoke to you this week?

2. What insights did you gain about God?

3. What application might this have to what is happening in the world today?

4. How would God have you apply this truth to your life?

Notes from Reflecting on This Week's Bible Readings

Week 38

What is God's prescription for bringing healing to our nation? Find out this week as we read the book of 2 Chronicles.

For an introduction to Song of Solomon, see appendix 1, page 399.

— DAY 1 —

Today's Reading: Song of Solomon 1–4

Verse of the Day:

How beautiful is your love, my sister, my bride!
    How much better is your love than wine,
    and the fragrance of your oils than any spice! — Song of Solomon 4:10

Questions for Reflection and Discussion

1. What mutual declaration did the lovers declare to each other (1:15–16)?

2. What is meant that Solomon's bride is like a locked garden (4:12)?
   a. She is inaccessible.
   b. She is a complete mystery.
   c. She is a chaste virgin.
   d. None of the above.

Notes on Today's Bible Reading

— DAY 2 —

Today's Reading: Song of Solomon 5–8

Verse of the Day:

Many waters cannot quench love,
    neither can floods drown it.
If a man offered for love
    all the wealth of his house,
    he would be utterly despised. — Song of Solomon 8:7

Questions for Reflection and Discussion

1. Watchmen on the walls had authority, but in Song 5:7, they abused the king's bride to be. Like believers throughout history, she was persecuted as she sought her beloved. The watchmen found her and:
    a. Beat her
    b. Bruised her
    c. Took away her veil
    d. All of the above

2. When Solomon wrote Song of Songs 6:8–9 he had "sixty queens and eighty concubines, and virgins without number" (which grew to seven hundred, three hundred, and still innumerable). Yet in verse 9, he calls his betrothed a "dove," "my perfect one," "the only one." Of whom was he speaking prophetically throughout this amazing God-breathed love story? (See 2 Cor. 11:2–3 and Eph. 5:27.)

Notes on Today's Bible Reading

_____

_____

_____

_____

_____

_____

_____

— DAY 3 —

Today's Reading: 2 Chronicles 1

For an introduction to 2 Chronicles, see appendix 1, page 400.

Verse of the Day:

"Give me now wisdom and knowledge to go out and come in before this people, for who can govern this people of yours, which is so great?" — 2 Chronicles 1:10

Questions for Reflection and Discussion

1. For what specific purpose did King Solomon ask God for wisdom?

2. What did God give Solomon that he didn't ask for?
   a. Riches
   b. Wealth
   c. Glory
   d. All of the above

Notes on Today's Bible Reading

— DAY 4 —

Today's Reading: 2 Chronicles 2–3

Verse of the Day:

Then Solomon began to build the house of the LORD in Jerusalem on Mount Moriah, where the LORD had appeared to David his father, at the place that David had appointed, on the threshing floor of Ornan the Jebusite. — 2 Chronicles 3:1

Questions for Reflection and Discussion

1. Why did Solomon tell King Hiram of Tyre he wanted to build God a great house, and yet what did Solomon conclude about God (2 Chron. 2:5–6)?

2. What was the primary precious metal that adorned the temple?
   a. Bronze
   b. Silver
   c. Platinum
   d. None of the above

Notes on Today's Bible Reading

— DAY 5 —

Today's Reading: 2 Chronicles 4–5

Verse of the Day:

([A]nd it was the duty of the trumpeters and singers to make themselves heard in unison in praise and thanksgiving to the LORD), and when the song was raised, with trumpets and cymbals and other musical instruments, in praise to the LORD,

"For he is good, for his steadfast love endures forever,"

the house, the house of the LORD, was filled with a cloud. — 2 Chronicles 5:13

Questions for Reflection and Discussion

1. Among the temple furnishings was a bronze altar, which was the first main object greeting the worshipper who entered the sanctuary court of the new temple. What does the altar signify?
   a. The altar was a receptacle for the worshipper's loose change.
   b. God expects a gift when entering his house.
   c. Holy God may only be approached through sacrifice.
   d. None of the above.

2. When the priests placed the ark of the covenant in the Most Holy Place, what prevented them from performing their duties (2 Chron. 5:13–14)?

Notes on Today's Bible Reading

Size comparison
(approximate):

Temple
Altar

Upper Court
(Inner Court)

**Priests' rooms
and storage**

American
Football Field

Great Court
(Outer Court)

**Holy
Place**

Great Court
(Outer Court)

Altar

Boaz

Great Court
(Outer Court)

Porch

Jachin

Ramp

**INSIDE
THE TEMPLE**
(cutaway view)

1. Holy of Holies
2. Cherubim
3. Ark of the Covenant
4. Veil
5. Altar of Incense
6. Table of Shewbread
7. Lampstand
8. Priests' rooms and storage

Lavers
and Bases

Upper Court
(Inner Court)

Molten
Sea

Great Court
(Outer Court)

Solomon's Temple

The First Temple, erected by King Solomon, was built to replace
the Tabernacle and to house the Ark of the Covenant. The
Temple was completed in 957 BC after seven years of labor,
but was destroyed by the Babylonians in 587 BC.

Great Court
(Outer Court)

GRAPHIC BY KARBEL MULTIMEDIA.
COPYRIGHT 2008 LOGOS BIBLE SOFTWARE

— DAY 6 —

Today's Reading: 2 Chronicles 6–7

Verse of the Day:

"But the LORD said to David my father, 'Whereas it was in your heart to build a house for My name, you did well that it was in your heart.'" — 2 Chronicles 6:8

Questions for Reflection and Discussion

1. What happened immediately following Solomon's prayer of dedication in 2 Chronicles 7:1–3?

2. When the nation experienced God's judgments as a result of their sin, on what conditions did the Lord promise to hear from heaven, forgive their sins, and heal their land?
    a. God's people must humble themselves before Him.
    b. God's people must pray and seek God's face.
    c. God's people must turn from their wicked ways.
    d. All of the above.

Notes on Today's Bible Reading

_____

_____

_____

_____

_____

_____

_____

_____

_____

_____

— DAY 7 —
Review of This Week's Readings:
Song of Solomon 1–8; 2 Chronicles 1–7

Questions for Reflection and Discussion

1. What passage uniquely spoke to you this week?

2. What insights did you gain about God?

3. What application might this have to what is happening in the world today?

4. How would God have you apply this truth to your life?

Notes from Reflecting on This Week's Bible Readings

Week 39

What does God promise He will do if we walk in His ways and obey His commandments? Find out as we read the book of 1 Kings this week.

— DAY 1 —
Today's Reading: 2 Chronicles 8–9

Verse of the Day:

Thus King Solomon excelled all the kings of the earth in riches and in wisdom. — 2 Chronicles 9:22

Questions for Reflection and Discussion

1. In chapter 8, why didn't Solomon want Pharaoh's daughter to live in the house of David (v. 11)?

2. In chapter 9, what impressed the queen of Sheba and whom did she credit (vv. 5–8)?

Notes on Today's Bible Reading

— DAY 2 —

Today's Reading: 1 Kings 3–4

Verse of the Day:

It pleased the Lord that Solomon had asked this. — 1 Kings 3:10

Questions for Reflection and Discussion

1. What did the Lord promise Solomon in addition to the wisdom he requested?
   a. Riches
   b. Honor
   c. Long life if he would walk as David walked, honoring God's word
   d. All of the above

2. Just how wise did Solomon become (4:29–34)?

Notes on Today's Bible Reading

— DAY 3 —

Today's Reading: 1 Kings 5–6

Verses of the Day:

Now the word of the LORD came to Solomon, "Concerning this house that you are building, if you will walk in my statutes and obey my rules and keep all my commandments and walk in them, then I will establish my word with you, which I spoke to David your father. And I will dwell among the children of Israel and will not forsake my people Israel." — 1 Kings 6:11–13

Questions for Reflection and Discussion

1. Why did the Lord choose Solomon, rather than his father, King David, to build the temple (5:2–5; 1 Chron. 22:8; 28:3)?

2. What were the conditions to be met by Solomon for the Lord to keep his promise to "establish my word with you, which I spoke to David your father" and to "dwell among the children of Israel and will not forsake my people Israel" (6:12–13)?

Notes on Today's Bible Reading

— DAY 4 —
Today's Reading: 1 Kings 7

Verse of the Day:

Thus all the work that King Solomon did on the house of the LORD was finished. And Solomon brought in the things that David his father had dedicated, the silver, the gold, and the vessels, and stored them in the treasuries of the house of the LORD. — 1 Kings 7:51

Questions for Reflection and Discussion

1. Once the temple was completed, Solomon built his own palace with the "Hall of the Throne." What was the purpose of this hall?

2. After Solomon completed the temple and its furnishings, what did he contribute to the treasuries of the Lord's temple?

Notes on Today's Bible Reading

— DAY 5 —
Today's Reading: 1 Kings 8

Verses of the Day:

"The Lord our God be with us, as he was with our fathers. May he not leave us or forsake us, that he may incline our hearts to him, to walk in all his ways and to keep his commandments, his statutes, and his rules, which he commanded our fathers." — 1 Kings 8:57–58

Questions for Reflection and Discussion

1. When the priests brought the ark of the Lord up from Zion, the city of David, to the Most Holy Place within the temple, what was inside of the ark?

2. In Solomon's prayer of dedication (vv. 22–53), what did he most earnestly desire of the Lord:
   a. Success and riches
   b. Comfort and security
   c. Mercy and forgiveness
   d. Fame and honor

Notes on Today's Bible Reading

— DAY 6 —
Today's Reading: 1 Kings 9–10

Verses of the Day:

"And this house will become a heap of ruins. Everyone passing by it will be astonished and will hiss, and they will say, 'Why has the LORD done thus to this land and to this house?' Then they will say, 'Because they abandoned the LORD their God who brought their fathers out of the land of Egypt and laid hold on other gods and worshiped them and served them. Therefore the LORD has brought all this disaster on them.'" — 1 Kings 9:8–9

Questions for Reflection and Discussion

1. In chapter 9, God makes an unconditional promise regarding Jerusalem but a conditional promise to Solomon. What were some of the conditions to God's continued blessing on Solomon and his descendants?
   a. Walk before me, as David walked, with integrity of heart and uprightness
   b. Do according to all that I have commanded
   c. Keep my statutes and my rules
   d. All of the above

2. In chapter 10, the queen of Sheba exclaimed, "Because the Lord loved _____ forever, he has made you king, that you may execute justice and righteousness."

Notes on Today's Bible Reading

_____

_____

_____

_____

_____

_____

_____

_____

— DAY 7 —
Review of This Week's Readings:
2 Chronicles 8–9; 1 Kings 3–10

Questions for Reflection and Discussion

1. What passage uniquely spoke to you this week?

2. What insights did you gain about God?

3. What application might this have to what is happening in the world today?

4. How would God have you apply this truth to your life?

Notes from Reflecting on This Week's Bible Readings

Week 40

What comfort can we find in our adversity? Find out as we begin Ecclesiastes this week.

— DAY 1 —

Today's Reading: 1 Kings 11

Verse of the Day:

For when Solomon was old his wives turned away his heart after other gods, and his heart was not wholly true to the LORD his God, as was the heart of David his father. — 1 Kings 11:4

Questions for Reflection and Discussion

1. Why was God displeased with Solomon?
2. As a result of Solomon's idolatry, what judgment came?

Notes on Today's Bible Reading

— DAY 2 —

Today's Reading: Ecclesiastes 1–2

For an introduction to Ecclesiastes, see appendix 1, page 402.

Verse of the Day:

Vanity of vanities, says the Preacher,
　　vanity of vanities! All is vanity. — Ecclesiastes 1:2

Questions for Reflection and Discussion

1. What word did Solomon (a.k.a. "the Preacher") use repeatedly to describe the fact that life without the Lord was a pointless pursuit?
　a. Immorality
　b. Insanity
　c. Vanity
　d. None of the above

2. After a cynical assessment of life's pursuits, Solomon nonetheless concluded that God blesses the person who is _____ in His view (Eccles. 2:26).

Notes on Today's Bible Reading

— DAY 3 —

Today's Reading: Ecclesiastes 3–4

Verse of the Day:

So I saw that there is nothing better than that a man should rejoice in his work, for that is his lot. Who can bring him to see what will be after him? — Ecclesiastes 3:22

Questions for Reflection and Discussion

1. In chapter 3, the Preacher declared that for everything there is a _____?

2. In 4:9–12, what was the point made?
   a. Two are better than one when it comes to labor.
   b. Going it alone can lead to trouble.
   c. Two can better defend against attack.
   d. All of the above.

Notes on Today's Bible Reading

— DAY 4 —

Today's Reading: Ecclesiastes 5–6

Verse of the Day:

He who loves money will not be satisfied with money, nor he who loves wealth with his income; this also is vanity. — Ecclesiastes 5:10

Questions for Reflection and Discussion

1. According to Ecclesiastes 5, when going to the house of God, it is important to:
   a. Avoid hasty words
   b. Guard your steps
   c. Go near to listen
   d. All of the above

2. According to Solomon (e.g., 5:10; 6:7), the love of money and the accumulation of wealth, regardless of motive, can never _____.

Notes on Today's Bible Reading

— DAY 5 —

Today's Reading: Ecclesiastes 7–8

Verse of the Day:

A good name is better than precious ointment,
and the day of death than the day of birth. — Ecclesiastes 7:1

Questions for Reflection and Discussion

1. In Ecclesiastes 7:20, Solomon claimed there is not a righteous or just man who does good who does not _____.

2. According to Solomon, what happens to people's hearts when the sentence for a crime is not carried out quickly (8:11)?

Notes on Today's Bible Reading

_____

_____

_____

_____

_____

_____

_____

_____

_____

_____

_____

_____

_____

— DAY 6 —

Today's Reading: Ecclesiastes 9–10

Verse of the Day:

A wise man's heart inclines him to the right, but a fool's heart to the left. — Ecclesiastes 10:2

Questions for Reflection and Discussion

1. In chapter 9, what is "the same event [that] happens to all" according to Solomon?
   a. Hair loss
   b. Weight gain
   c. Wrinkles
   d. Death

2. What does a little folly overpower (10:1–2)?

Notes on Today's Bible Reading

— DAY 7 —

Review of This Week's Readings:
1 Kings 11; Ecclesiastes 1–10

Questions for Reflection and Discussion

1. What passage uniquely spoke to you this week?

2. What insights did you gain about God?

3. What application might this have to what is happening in the world today?

4. How would God have you apply this truth to your life?

Notes from Reflecting on This Week's Bible Readings

_____

_____

_____

_____

_____

_____

_____

_____

_____

_____

_____

_____

_____

_____

What encouragement do we have when facing life's battles? Find out as we continue the book of 2 Chronicles this week.

— DAY 1 —

Today's Reading: Ecclesiastes 11–12

Verses of the Day:

The end of the matter; all has been heard. Fear God and keep his commandments, for this is the whole duty of man. For God will bring every deed into judgment, with every secret thing, whether good or evil. — Ecclesiastes 12:13–14

Questions for Reflection and Discussion

1. What is the principle being taught in 11:1–2?
   a. Nothing ventured nothing gained.
   b. Better late than never.
   c. Generosity often comes back around to us.
   d. None of the above.

2. What is the whole duty of every person according to 12:13?

Notes on Today's Bible Reading

_____

_____

_____

_____

_____

_____

_____

_____

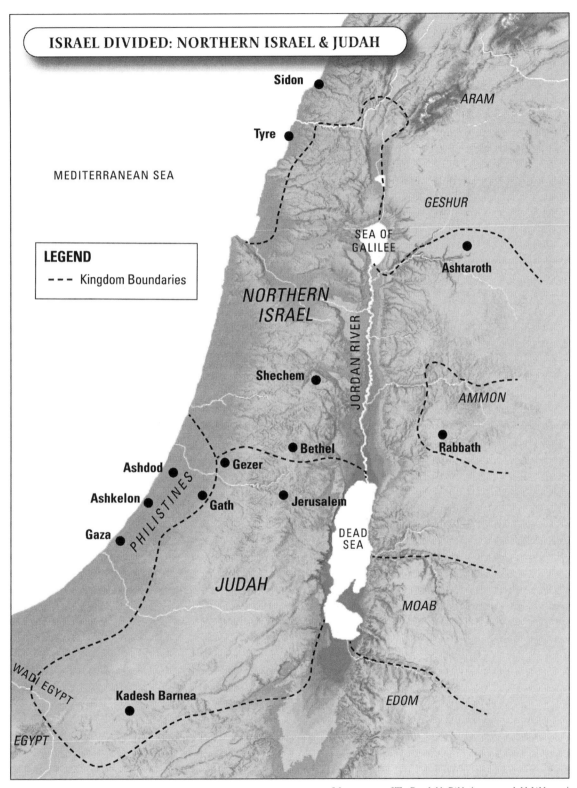

ISRAEL DIVIDED: NORTHERN ISRAEL & JUDAH

Sidon

ARAM

Tyre

MEDITERRANEAN SEA

GESHUR

SEA OF
GALILEE

Ashtaroth

LEGEND
- - - Kingdom Boundaries

NORTHERN
ISRAEL

JORDAN RIVER

AMMON

Shechem

Bethel

Rabbath

Ashdod

Gezer

PHILISTINES

Ashkelon

Gath

Jerusalem

Gaza

DEAD
SEA

JUDAH

MOAB

WADI EGYPT

Kadesh Barnea

EDOM

EGYPT

Map courtesy of The Readable Bible (www.readablebible.com)

— DAY 2 —

Today's Reading: 2 Chronicles 10–12

Verse of the Day:

Then the princes of Israel and the king humbled themselves and said, "The Lord is righteous." — 2 Chronicles 12:6

Questions for Reflection and Discussion

1. What led to the division of the nation of Israel (10:1–15)?
   a. King Rehoboam did not listen to the older advisers who counseled him to lighten the people's burden.
   b. Rehoboam did listen to the younger advisers who counseled that he increase their burden.
   c. God influenced the outcome in fulfillment of predictive prophecy.
   d. All of the above.

2. What was the result of all the worshippers of the Lord leaving the idol-worshipping kingdom of Israel under Jeroboam and migrating south to the kingdom of Judah (11:13–17)?

Notes on Today's Bible Reading

— DAY 3 —

Today's Reading: 2 Chronicles 13–16

Verse of the Day:

[A]nd he went out to meet Asa and said to him, "Hear me, Asa, and all Judah and Benjamin: The LORD is with you while you are with him. If you seek him, he will be found by you, but if you forsake him, he will forsake you." — 2 Chronicles 15:2

Questions for Reflection and Discussion

1. Why did God prosper King Asa and give him victory in battle at the beginning of his reign (14:1–3)?
   a. He took away the pagan altars, broke down the pillars, and cut down the idols.
   b. He commanded Judah to seek the Lord, the God of their fathers, and to keep the law and the commandment.
   c. He took out the idolatrous high places and the incense altars from all the cities of Judah.
   d. All of the above.

2. According to 16:9, why do the eyes of the Lord range throughout the earth?

Notes on Today's Bible Reading

_____

_____

_____

_____

_____

_____

_____

_____

_____

— DAY 4 —

Today's Reading: 2 Chronicles 17–18

Verses of the Day:

The LORD was with Jehoshaphat, because he walked in the earlier ways of his father David. He did not seek the Baals, but sought the God of his father and walked in his commandments, and not according to the practices of Israel. — 2 Chronicles 17:3–4

Questions for Reflection and Discussion

1. In the third year of his reign, Jehoshaphat sent his officials, along with Levites and priests, throughout Judah to instruct the people. According to 17:7–10, what did they teach, and what was the result?

2. When Jehoshaphat, king of Judah, unwisely allied himself with Ahab, king of Israel, for a joint military operation against a common enemy, what did Jehoshaphat insist they do before they made their move (18:4)?

Notes on Today's Bible Reading

— DAY 5 —

Today's Reading: 2 Chronicles 19–20

Verse of the Day:

O our God, will you not execute judgment on them? For we are powerless against this great horde that is coming against us. We do not know what to do, but our eyes are on you." — 2 Chronicles 20:12

Questions for Reflection and Discussion

1. According to 19:1–2 and 20:35–37, what did King Jehoshaphat do to bring the wrath of God upon him?

2. When surrounded by a vast enemy army, King Jehoshaphat humbled himself, proclaimed a fast, and cried out to the Lord (20:1–23): "We do not know what to do, but our eyes are on you" (v. 12). Following this expression of dependence on the Lord, what did the prophet Jahaziel prophesy?
   a. The battle is not yours but God's.
   b. Stand firm and see the salvation of the Lord on your behalf.
   c. Tomorrow go out against them, and the Lord will be with you.
   d. All of the above.

Notes on Today's Bible Reading

— DAY 6 —

Today's Reading: 2 Chronicles 21–23

Verses of the Day:

Jehoram was thirty-two years old when he became king, and he reigned eight years in Jerusalem. And he walked in the way of the kings of Israel, as the house of Ahab had done, for the daughter of Ahab was his wife. And he did what was evil in the sight of the LORD." — 2 Chronicles 21:5–6

Questions for Reflection and Discussion

1. What did Jehoram do with his brothers when he became king of Judah (21:4)?
   a. Invited them to a party
   b. Let them try out his crown
   c. Put them to death
   d. None of the above

2. How long was Joash hidden in the temple of God while the wicked Queen Athaliah ruled? (22:11–12)?

Notes on Today's Bible Reading

— DAY 7 —
Review of This Week's Readings:
Ecclesiastes 11–12; 2 Chronicles 10–23

Questions for Reflection and Discussion

1. What passage uniquely spoke to you this week?

2. What insights did you gain about God?

3. What application might this have to what is happening in the world today?

4. How would God have you apply this truth to your life?

Notes from Reflecting on This Week's Bible Readings

What discovery led to national repentance? Find out as we conclude 2 Chronicles.

— DAY 1 —

Today's Reading: 2 Chronicles 24–25

Verse of the Day:

Joash did what was right in the eyes of the LORD all the days of Jehoiada the priest. — 2 Chronicles 24:2

Questions for Reflection and Discussion

1. What did King Joash command to be done to Zechariah, son of Jehoaida, who prophesied against him? (24:19–22)?

2. After Amaziah defeated the Edomites, what did he do with their gods (25:14–16)?
   a. Mocked them
   b. Removed them
   c. Worshipped them
   d. None of the above

Notes on Today's Bible Reading

— DAY 2 —

Today's Reading: 2 Chronicles 26–28

Verses of the Day:

But Azariah the priest went in after him, with eighty priests of the LORD who were men of valor, and they withstood King Uzziah and said to him, "It is not for you, Uzziah, to burn incense to the LORD, but for the priests, the sons of Aaron, who are consecrated to burn incense. Go out of the sanctuary, for you have done wrong, and it will bring you no honor from the LORD God. — 2 Chronicles 26:17–18

Questions for Reflection and Discussion

1. What did King Uzziah do that brought God's swift and severe judgment?
   a. Put a prophet in jail because he didn't like the message
   b. Performed a function reserved for a priest
   c. Worshipped idols rather than the one true God
   d. None of the above

2. Why did God deliver King Ahaz into the hands of his enemies (28:2–5)?

Notes on Today's Bible Reading

— DAY 3 —
Today's Reading: 2 Chronicles 29–30

Verse of the Day:

Then Hezekiah the king rose early and gathered the officials of the city and went up to the house of the Lord. — 2 Chronicles 29:20

Questions for Reflection and Discussion

1. When Hezekiah took the throne, what immediate initiatives did he set in motion to lead the people in a return to the one true God?
   a. Removed the heathen high places of worship, broke up the pagan pillars, and cut down the idols
   b. Reopened the temple, cleaned out all the filth, and ordered that worship of the one true God begin again
   c. Renewed their celebration of the Passover
   d. All of the above

2. King Hezekiah invited all Israel (northern and southern kingdoms) to celebrate the Passover. What promises did he make to the northern kingdom Israelites if they would return and yield themselves to the Lord God (30:9)?

Notes on Today's Bible Reading

_____

_____

_____

_____

_____

_____

_____

_____

— DAY 4 —

Today's Reading: 2 Chronicles 31–32

Verses of the Day:

"Be strong and courageous. Do not be afraid or dismayed before the king of Assyria and all the horde that is with him, for there are more with us than with him. With him is an arm of flesh, but with us is the LORD our God, to help us and to fight our battles." And the people took confidence from the words of Hezekiah king of Judah. — 2 Chronicles 32:7–8

Questions for Reflection and Discussion

1. After celebrating the Passover, what were the people of both Israel and Judah inspired to do as they returned home (31:1)?

2. When a massive Assyrian army, led by a blaspheming Sennacherib, laid siege to Judah's fortified cities, after having already carried away the northern kingdom captive, what did King Hezekiah tell his people (32:7–8)?
   a. Run for your lives; there is no way we can stop them!
   b. Hide in your homes; maybe they won't find you!
   c. With us is the Lord our God, to help us and to fight our battles!
   d. None of the above.

Notes on Today's Bible Reading

_____

_____

_____

_____

_____

_____

_____

— DAY 5 —

Today's Reading: 2 Chronicles 33

Verses of the Day:

The LORD spoke to Manasseh and to his people, but they paid no attention. Therefore the LORD brought upon them the commanders of the army of the king of Assyria, who captured Manasseh with hooks and bound him with chains of bronze and brought him to Babylon. And when he was in distress, he entreated the favor of the LORD his God and humbled himself greatly before the God of his fathers. He prayed to him, and God was moved by his entreaty and heard his plea and brought him again to Jerusalem into his kingdom. Then Manasseh knew that the LORD was God. — 2 Chronicles 33:10–13

Questions for Reflection and Discussion

1. King Manasseh caused the people of Judah to do more evil than the heathen nations God destroyed in the land as they entered. Yet we read that Manasseh humbled himself and led a return to the Lord (33:13, 15–16). What events led to his change of heart (33:10–12)?
   a. God sent the Assyrian army to invade.
   b. The Assyrians captured Manasseh and put him in chains.
   c. Manasseh was taken to Babylon as a captive.
   d. All of the above.

2. What discovery in the eighteenth year of Josiah's reign led to national repentance and wholehearted commitment to God's covenant (34:14–33)?

Notes on Today's Bible Reading

— DAY 6 —

Today's Reading: 2 Chronicles 34–36

Verses of the Day:

The Lord, the God of their fathers, sent persistently to them by his messengers, because he had compassion on his people and on his dwelling place. But they kept mocking the messengers of God, despising his words and scoffing at his prophets, until the wrath of the Lord rose against his people, until there was no remedy. — 2 Chronicles 36:15–16

Questions for Reflection and Discussion

1. What special celebration did the godly King Josiah reinstitute in chapter 35?
   a. Feast of Tabernacles
   b. Feast of Trumpets
   c. Feast of Passover
   d. None of the above

2. After the sad demise of the kingdom of Judah—because of God's judgment through the invasion of King Nebuchadnezzar and the captivity in Babylon—how does the book of 2 Chronicles end (36:15–23)?

Notes on Today's Bible Reading

_____

_____

_____

_____

_____

_____

_____

_____

— DAY 7 —
Review of This Week's Readings:
2 Chronicles 24–36

Questions for Reflection and Discussion

1. What passage uniquely spoke to you this week?

2. What insights did you gain about God?

3. What application might this have to what is happening in the world today?

4. How would God have you apply this truth to your life?

Notes from Reflecting on This Week's Bible Readings

Week 43

What does effective prayer look like? Find out this week as we continue through 1 Kings.

— DAY 1 —

Today's Reading: 1 Kings 12–13

Verse of the Day:

"If you will be a servant to this people today and serve them, and speak good words to them when you answer them, then they will be your servants forever." — 1 Kings 12:7

Questions for Reflection and Discussion

1. In chapter 12, what did King Jeroboam refer to when he declared, "Behold your gods, O Israel, who brought you up out of the land of Egypt"?

2. In chapter 13, what happened to Jeroboam when he stretched out his hand against the prophet who spoke judgment against his pagan altar? What happened to it when the prophet prayed for him?

Notes on Today's Bible Reading

— DAY 2 —

Today's Reading: 1 Kings 14–15

Verse of the Day:

He did what was evil in the sight of the LORD and walked in the way of his father, and in his sin which he made Israel to sin. — 1 Kings 15:26

Questions for Reflection and Discussion

1. In chapter 14, what did Ahijah the prophet foretell would happen to Jeroboam's sons?

2. In chapter 15, what did King Asa do that was right in the eyes of the Lord (vv. 12–13), and what did he leave undone (v. 14)?

Notes on Today's Bible Reading

— DAY 3 —

Today's Reading: 1 Kings 16–17

Verses of the Day:

And Elijah said to her, "Do not fear; go and do as you have said. But first make me a little cake of it and bring it to me, and afterward make something for yourself and your son. For thus says the LORD, the God of Israel, 'The jar of flour shall not be spent, and the jug of oil shall not be empty, until the day that the LORD sends rain upon the earth.'" And she went and did as Elijah said. And she and he and her household ate for many days. — 1 Kings 17:13–15

Questions for Reflection and Discussion

1. According to 1 Kings 16, what did Ahab do that made him more evil than all the kings before him?
   a. Married Jezebel, wicked daughter of the king of Sidon
   b. Served and worshipped the false god Baal
   c. Constructed an Asherah pole for pagan worship
   d. All of the above

2. Compare 1 Kings 17:1 to James 5:16–17. What do these verses tell us about Elijah's prayers? And our prayers?

Notes on Today's Bible Reading

Timeline of Kings and Prophets

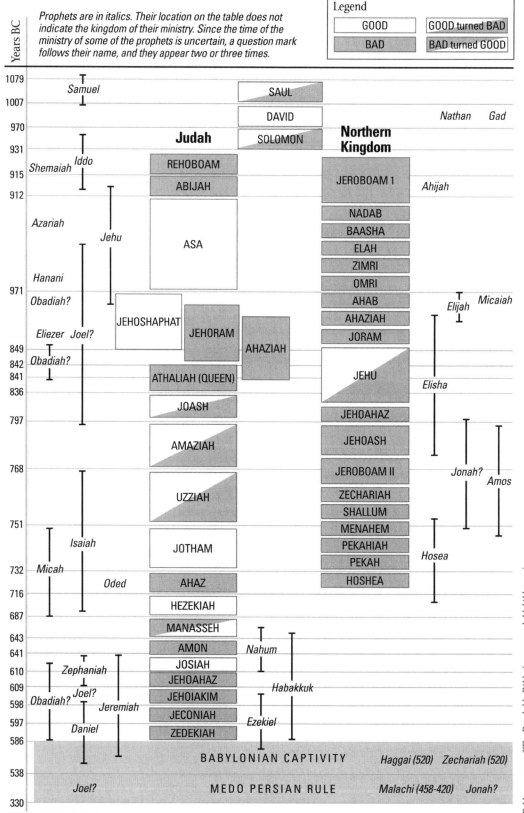

Prophets are in italics. Their location on the table does not indicate the kingdom of their ministry. Since the time of the ministry of some of the prophets is uncertain, a question mark follows their name, and they appear two or three times.

Legend

GOOD	GOOD turned BAD
BAD	BAD turned GOOD

Years BC

1079	*Samuel*	SAUL
1007		DAVID
970		*Nathan* *Gad*
931	**Judah** SOLOMON	**Northern Kingdom**
915	*Shemaiah* *Iddo* REHOBOAM	JEROBOAM 1
912	ABIJAH	*Ahijah*
	Azariah	NADAB
		BAASHA
	Jehu ASA	ELAH
		ZIMRI
	Hanani	OMRI
971	*Obadiah?*	AHAB *Elijah* *Micaiah*
	JEHOSHAPHAT JEHORAM	AHAZIAH
	Eliezer *Joel?*	JORAM
849		
842	*Obadiah?* AHAZIAH	JEHU *Elisha*
841	ATHALIAH (QUEEN)	
836	JOASH	
797		JEHOAHAZ
768	AMAZIAH	JEHOASH
	UZZIAH	JEROBOAM II *Jonah?* *Amos*
		ZECHARIAH
751		SHALLUM
	Isaiah JOTHAM	MENAHEM
		PEKAHIAH
732	*Micah*	PEKAH *Hosea*
716	*Oded* AHAZ	HOSHEA
687	HEZEKIAH	
643	MANASSEH	
641	AMON	*Nahum*
610	*Zephaniah* JOSIAH	
609	*Joel?* JEHOAHAZ	*Habakkuk*
598	*Obadiah?* JEHOIAKIM *Jeremiah*	
597	*Daniel* JECONIAH	*Ezekiel*
586	ZEDEKIAH	
538	BABYLONIAN CAPTIVITY	*Haggai (520)* *Zechariah (520)*
330	*Joel?* MEDO PERSIAN RULE	*Malachi (458-420)* *Jonah?*

Table courtesy of The Readable Bible (www.readablebible.com)

308

— DAY 4 —

Today's Reading: 1 Kings 18–19

Verse of the Day:

Then Elijah said to the prophets of Baal, "Choose for yourselves one bull and prepare it first, for you are many, and call upon the name of your god, but put no fire to it." — 1 Kings 18:25

Questions for Reflection and Discussion

1. According to 1 Kings 18, what happened on Mount Carmel when the prophets of Baal offered a sacrifice to their god, cut themselves, and cried out until they were hoarse? What happened when Elijah offered a sacrifice and prayed to the Lord? What was the response of the people?

2. After the great victory on Mount Carmel, Elijah fled for his life from Jezebel in chapter 19. How did the Lord reveal Himself to the depressed prophet on Mount Horeb?
   a. Wind that tore the mountains
   b. Earthquake that shook the ground
   c. Fire that burned
   d. Gentle whisper
   e. All of the above

Notes on Today's Bible Reading

— DAY 5 —

Today's Reading: 1 Kings 20–21

Verses of the Day:

And the word of the LORD came to Elijah the Tishbite, saying, "Have you seen how Ahab has humbled himself before me? Because he has humbled himself before me, I will not bring the disaster in his days; but in his son's days I will bring the disaster upon his house." — 1 Kings 21:28–29

Questions for Reflection and Discussion

1. Why did the prophet of the Lord announce severe judgment upon Ahab and his people after God gave him victory over Ben-hadad, king of Syria (20:35–42)?

2. According to 1 Kings 21:25, "There was none who sold himself to do what was evil in the sight of the Lord like Ahab" because he listened to his wicked wife, Jezebel. Yet when Ahab heard the words of the prophet Elijah foretelling his death and the death of his wife, what did he do (v. 27)? And what did the Lord do as a result (vv. 28–29)?

Notes on Today's Bible Reading

— DAY 6 —

Today's Reading: 1 Kings 22

Verses of the Day:

And the messenger who went to summon Micaiah said to him, "Behold, the words of the prophets with one accord are favorable to the king. Let your word be like the word of one of them, and speak favorably." But Micaiah said, "As the LORD lives, what the LORD says to me, that I will speak." — 1 Kings 22:13–14

Questions for Reflection and Discussion

1. Why did King Ahab not want to consult a true prophet of God concerning a proposed joint military operation with King Jehoshaphat of Judah?
    a. Ahab believed the prophet Micaiah hated him because he spoke God's truth.
    b. Ahab wanted only to hear encouragement from his court prophets who predicted victory.
    c. Ahab feared a negative word would come from God's prophet because of his guilt associated with leading Israel into idolatry.
    d. All of the above.

2. What happened to Ahab after jailing Micaiah for his prophecy?

Notes on Today's Bible Reading

_____

_____

_____

_____

_____

_____

_____

_____

_____

— DAY 7 —
Review of This Week's Readings:
1 Kings 12–22

Questions for Reflection and Discussion

1. What passage uniquely spoke to you this week?

2. What insights did you gain about God?

3. What application might this have to what is happening in the world today?

4. How would God have you apply this truth to your life?

Notes from Reflecting on This Week's Bible Readings

Why do Christians need not be afraid even when surrounded by the enemy? Find out this week as we read 2 Kings.

For an introduction to 2 Kings, see appendix 1, page 403.

— DAY 1 —
Today's Reading: 2 Kings 1–2

Verse of the Day:

And as they still went on and talked, behold, chariots of fire and horses of fire separated the two of them. And Elijah went up by a whirlwind into heaven. — 2 Kings 2:11

Questions for Reflection and Discussion

1. What happed to the first two military units King Ahaziah sent to apprehend the prophet Elijah? What happened to the third unit, and why were they spared?

2. Why did Elijah discourage Elisha from continuing to accompany him on his journeys?
    a. Elijah could travel more quickly alone.
    b. Elijah was concerned about the extra expense.
    c. Elijah was testing Elisha.
    d. None of the above.

Notes on Today's Bible Reading

— DAY 2 —

Today's Reading: 2 Kings 3–4

Verse of the Day:

And Jehoshaphat said, "Is there no prophet of the LORD here, through whom we may inquire of the LORD?" Then one of the king of Israel's servants answered, "Elisha the son of Shaphat is here, who poured water on the hands of Elijah." — 2 Kings 3:11

Questions for Reflection and Discussion

1. While the prophet Elisha had regard for King Jehoshaphat in chapter 3, what was his stance toward Jehoram, son of Ahab and king of Israel?

2. How was Elisha able to repay the Shunammite woman's hospitality?

Notes on Today's Bible Reading

— DAY 3 —

Today's Reading: 2 Kings 5–6

Verses of the Day:

He said, "Do not be afraid, for those who are with us are more than those who are with them." Then Elisha prayed and said, "O Lord, please open his eyes that he may see." So the Lord opened the eyes of the young man, and he saw, and behold, the mountain was full of horses and chariots of fire all around Elisha. — 2 Kings 6:16–17

Questions for Reflection and Discussion

1. When Naaman, commander of the Syrian army, came to the prophet Elisha to be healed of his leprosy, how did he react when Elisha told him to dip seven times in the Jordan River and he would be restored? Once he humbled himself and did so, what was his confession (5:11, 15)?

2. According to 2 Kings 6, when chariots and horses of the Syrian army surrounded the city of Dothan, what did Elisha say to his fearful servant who was with him in the city (v. 16)? And what did his servant ultimately see (v. 17)?

Notes on Today's Bible Reading

— DAY 4 —
Today's Reading: 2 Kings 7–8

Verses of the Day:

For the Lord had made the army of the Syrians hear the sound of chariots and of horses, the sound of a great army, so that they said to one another, "Behold, the king of Israel has hired against us the kings of the Hittites and the kings of Egypt to come against us." So they fled away in the twilight and abandoned their tents, their horses, and their donkeys, leaving the camp as it was, and fled for their lives. — 2 Kings 7:6–7

Questions for Reflection and Discussion

1. What caused four desperate Jewish lepers to go to the camp of the Syrian army during the famine in Samaria (7:3–4)? What did they discover, and what caused the Syrian army to abandon camp (vv. 5–7)?

2. According to 2 Kings 8:4, Elisha's servant told the king of Israel about the great things Elisha had done. As the servant was speaking of the Shunammite widow whose son Elisha restored to life, who should appear? Explain the significance of the miraculous timing (vv. 5–6).

Notes on Today's Bible Reading

— DAY 5 —

Today's Reading: 2 Kings 9–10

Verses of the Day:

Thus Jehu wiped out Baal from Israel. But Jehu did not turn aside from the sins of Jeroboam the son of Nebat, which he made Israel sin—that is, the golden calves that were at Bethel and in Dan. — 2 Kings 10:28–29

Questions for Reflection and Discussion

1. Elisha instructed one among the company of prophets to go to Ramoth-gilead and anoint Jehu, a commander in the army, as king over Israel. What mission did the Lord give to Jehu (9:6–10)?

2. According to 2 Kings 10, after Jehu slaughtered all the house of Ahab in fulfillment of Elijah's prophecy (1 Kings 21:21–23), what further actions did he take to cleanse the land (10:18–28)?

Notes on Today's Bible Reading

— DAY 6 —

Today's Reading: 2 Kings 11–12

Verse of the Day:

And Jehoash did what was right in the eyes of the LORD all his days, because Jehoiada the priest instructed him. — 2 Kings 12:2

Questions for Reflection and Discussion

1. In chapter 11, what did Athaliah, the wicked daughter of Ahab and Jezebel, do upon the death of her son Ahaziah, king of Judah? What ultimately happened to her?

2. What was the deciding factor in making the reign of King Jehoash pleasing to God (12:2)?

Notes on Today's Bible Reading

— DAY 7 —
Review of This Week's Readings:
2 Kings 1–12

Questions for Reflection and Discussion

1. What passage uniquely spoke to you this week?

2. What insights did you gain about God?

3. What application might this have to what is happening in the world today?

4. How would God have you apply this truth to your life?

Notes from Reflecting on This Week's Bible Readings

Week 45

How should we treat the poor and oppressed? Find out this week as we read the book of Amos.

— DAY 1 —
Today's Reading: 2 Kings 13–14

Verses of the Day:

And Elisha said to him, "Take a bow and arrows." So he took a bow and arrows. Then he said to the king of Israel, "Draw the bow," and he drew it. And Elisha laid his hands on the king's hands. — 2 Kings 13:15–16

Questions for Reflection and Discussion

1. Why was the prophet Elisha angered that King Jehoash only struck three times with the arrows (13:19)?

2. In chapter 14, what was the parable that Jehoash, king of Israel, used to demean Amaziah, king of Judah, but also to discourage a confrontation?
   a. Parable of the sower and the soils
   b. Parable of the wheat and tares
   c. Parable of the thistle and the cedar
   d. None of the above

Notes on Today's Bible Reading

For an introduction to Joel, see appendix 1, page 404.

— DAY 2 —

Today's Reading: Joel 1

Verse of the Day:

Consecrate a fast;
    call a solemn assembly.
Gather the elders
    and all the inhabitants of the land
to the house of the Lord your God,
    and cry out to the Lord. — Joel 1:14

Questions for Reflection and Discussion

1. The prophet Joel called the elders and all the people to hear and recount the story of God's terrible judgments to succeeding generations (v. 3), but in what forms was the judgment coming?
   a. Plague of locusts
   b. Invading armies
   c. Famine
   d. All of the above

2. What did the prophet urgently call upon the priests to do in response to the relentless wave of God's remedial judgments?

Notes on Today's Bible Reading

— DAY 3 —

Today's Reading: Joel 2–3

Verse of the Day:

The LORD utters his voice
　　before his army,
for his camp is exceedingly great;
　　he who executes his word is powerful.
For the day of the LORD is great and very awesome;
　　who can endure it? — Joel 2:11

Questions for Reflection and Discussion

1. Following His devastating judgments and call for solemn assembly in chapters 1 and 2, what was God's word to Judah about the future (2:18–32)?
    a. Expect no pity from me
    b. Expect starvation
    c. Expect to remain a reproach
    d. Expect enemy occupation
    e. None of the above

2. Looking forward in time toward the final Day of the Lord, what did God say to the nations who were mistreating His people (3:9–16)?

Notes on Today's Bible Reading

For an introduction to Amos, see appendix 1, page 406.

— DAY 4 —

Today's Reading: Amos 1–2

Verse of the Day:

And he said:
> "The Lord roars from Zion
>   and utters his voice from Jerusalem;
> the pastures of the shepherds mourn,
>   and the top of Carmel withers." — Amos 1:2

Questions for Reflection and Discussion

1. According to Amos 1, what were the cruel sins against humanity that brought judgment upon Israel's neighbors, including Damascus, Gaza, Tyre, Edom, and Ammon?
   a. Threshing the captives of Gilead with sledges of iron
   b. Selling whole communities of captives to Edom, disregarding the covenant of brotherhood
   c. Stifling all compassion
   d. Ripping open the pregnant women of Gilead (as they extended their borders)
   e. All of the above

2. What command did backslidden Israel give to her prophets (2:12)?

Notes on Today's Bible Reading

_____

_____

_____

_____

_____

_____

_____

_____

_____

_____

_____

— DAY 5 —

Today's Reading: Amos 3–5

Verse of the Day:

"For the Lord God does nothing
without revealing his secret
to his servants the prophets." — Amos 3:7

Questions for Reflection and Discussion

1. Surely the sovereign Lord does _____ without revealing His plan to His servants the prophets (3:7).

2. According to chapter 5, even in the midst of pronouncements of judgments, what words of hope did Amos repeat during his lamentation over Israel (vv. 5, 6, 14, and 24)?

Notes on Today's Bible Reading

— DAY 6 —

Today's Reading: Amos 6–7

Verses of the Day:

And Amaziah said to Amos, "O seer, go, flee away to the land of Judah, and eat bread there, and prophesy there, but never again prophesy at Bethel, for it is the king's sanctuary, and it is a temple of the kingdom." — Amos 7:12–13

Questions for Reflection and Discussion

1. What was God's judgment on Israel's decadent lifestyle and arrogant attitude at the root of their injustice (6:7–8)?

2. What vision of coming destruction did God show Amos?
   a. Swarming locusts
   b. Devouring fire
   c. Hanging plumb line
   d. All of the above

Notes on Today's Bible Reading

— DAY 7 —
Review of This Week's Readings:
2 Kings 13–14; Joel 1–3; Amos 1–7

Questions for Reflection and Discussion

1. What passage uniquely spoke to you this week?

2. What insights did you gain about God?

3. What application might this have to what is happening in the world today?

4. How would God have you apply this truth to your life?

Notes from Reflecting on This Week's Bible Readings

When someone is unfaithful,
it hurts. Find out how God feels
in Hosea.

— DAY 1 —

Today's Reading: Amos 8–9

Verse of the Day:

"Behold, the days are coming," declares the Lord God,
   "when I will send a famine on the land—
not a famine of bread, nor a thirst for water,
   but of hearing the words of the Lord." — Amos 8:11

Questions for Reflection and Discussion

1. What coming famine did Amos announce that was not a famine of food or water?

2. After all the bleak judgment Amos pronounced, his prophecy ended with what promise from God?
   a. Reinstall a descendant of David to the throne
   b. Restore the fruitfulness of the land
   c. Return the exiles to the land
   d. All of the above

Notes on Today's Bible Reading

_____

_____

_____

_____

_____

_____

_____

— DAY 2 —

Today's Reading: Jonah 1–4

For an introduction to Jonah, see appendix 1, page 407.

Verse of the Day:

"And should not I pity Nineveh, that great city, in which there are more than 120,000 persons who do not know their right hand from their left, and also much cattle?" — Jonah 4:11

Questions for Reflection and Discussion

1. What did God send to swallow the disobedient prophet?
   a. Sea monster
   b. Whale
   c. Fish
   d. None of the above

2. What reason did God give Jonah for sparing the pagan people in Nineveh (4:11)?

Notes on Today's Bible Reading

For an introduction to Hosea, see appendix 1, page 409.

— DAY 3 —
Today's Reading: Hosea 1–3

Verses of the Day:

And the Lord said to me, "Go again, love a woman who is loved by another man and is an adulteress, even as the Lord loves the children of Israel, though they turn to other gods and love cakes of raisins." So I bought her for fifteen shekels of silver and a homer and a lethech of barley. — Hosea 3:1–2

Questions for Reflection and Discussion

1. According to chapter 1, why did the prophet Hosea marry an adulterous wife, Gomer? What was the significance of his children's names (vv. 4, 6, 9)?

2. What message is God giving to His people through Hosea's redemption of Gomer in chapter 3?

Notes on Today's Bible Reading

— DAY 4 —

Today's Reading: Hosea 4–5

Verse of the Day:

My people are destroyed for lack of knowledge;
  because you have rejected knowledge,
    I reject you from being a priest to me.
And since you have forgotten the law of your God,
  I also will forget your children. — Hosea 4:6

Questions for Reflection and Discussion

1. According to chapter 4, God brought charges against Israel, but who did God hold specifically responsible for the lack of knowledge that caused the people to perish (vv. 5–7)?

2. When Israel and Judah experienced God's disciplinary judgments but turned to Assyria for help, prompting further judgment, what was God still waiting for His people to do (5:15)?
   a. Admit their guilt
   b. Seek His face in their distress
   c. Earnestly seek Him
   d. All of the above

Notes on Today's Bible Reading

— DAY 5 —

Today's Reading: Hosea 6–8

Verses of the Day:

Because Ephraim has multiplied altars for sinning,
    they have become to him altars for sinning.
Were I to write for him my laws by the ten thousands,
    they would be regarded as a strange thing. — Hosea 8:11–12

Questions for Reflection and Discussion

1. The Lord longed to redeem His people, but what kept Him from doing so (7:13)?
   a. They spoke lies against the Lord.
   b. They did not cry to Him from the heart but wailed upon their beds.
   c. They plotted evil against the Lord.
   d. They did not turn to the Most High.
   e. All of the above.

2. What does Hosea say about sowing and reaping (8:7), and what is the implication for Israel?

Notes on Today's Bible Reading

_____

_____

_____

_____

_____

_____

_____

_____

_____

_____

— DAY 6 —

Today's Reading: Hosea 9–10

Verse of the Day:

Rejoice not, O Israel!
　　Exult not like the peoples;
for you have played the whore, forsaking your God.
　　You have loved a prostitute's wages
　　on all threshing floors. — Hosea 9:1

Questions for Reflection and Discussion

1. What was Israel like to God at the beginning of the relationship (9:10–13)?
   a. Grapes in the wilderness
   b. First fruit on the fig tree
   c. Young palm planted in a meadow
   d. All of the above

2. What do you think God means by the analogy in His command to "break up your fallow ground" in 10:12?

Notes on Today's Bible Reading

— DAY 7 —
Review of This Week's Readings:
Amos 8–9; Jonah 1–4; Hosea 1–10

Questions for Reflection and Discussion

1. What passage uniquely spoke to you this week?

2. What insights did you gain about God?

3. What application might this have to what is happening in the world today?

4. How would God have you apply this truth to your life?

Notes from Reflecting on This Week's Bible Readings

How does God respond to ingratitude in view of His abundant blessings? Find out this week as we begin Isaiah.

— DAY 1 —

Today's Reading: Hosea 11–14

Verse of the Day:

Whoever is wise, let him understand these things;
whoever is discerning, let him know them;
for the ways of the LORD are right,
and the upright walk in them,
but transgressors stumble in them. — Hosea 14:9

Questions for Reflection and Discussion

1. Hosea 11:1 is quoted in the New Testament. To whom is it applied? (Hint: Matthew 2)

2. What illustration did Hosea use to describe the nation's dim prospects under God's wrath (13:3)?
    a. Morning mist
    b. Dew that goes away
    c. Chaff that swirls from the threshing floor
    d. Smoke from a window
    e. All of the above

Notes on Today's Bible Reading

— DAY 2 —
Today's Reading: 2 Kings 15–16

Verse of the Day:

And he did what was right in the eyes of the LORD, according to all that his father Amaziah had done. — 2 Kings 15:3

Questions for Reflection and Discussion

1. What ongoing religious practice of the people did Jotham leave unchallenged in 15:34–35? What was the spiritual problem with this practice?

2. Besides the sacrifices in the high places, which had been going on for generations, what abominable pagan practice did King Ahaz add in 16:3?

Notes on Today's Bible Reading

_____

_____

_____

_____

_____

_____

_____

_____

_____

_____

_____

_____

_____

_____

For an introduction
to Isaiah,
see appendix 1,
page 410.

— DAY 3 —

Today's Reading: Isaiah 1–2

Verse of the Day:

"Come now, let us reason together, says the Lord:
though your sins are like scarlet,
    they shall be as white as snow;
though they are red like crimson,
    they shall become like wool." — Isaiah 1:18

Questions for Reflection and Discussion

1. God hated the sins and rebellion of His people so much that He rejected their insincere religious acts. Which did He name specifically (1:11–15)?
   a. Sermons
   b. Missions giving
   c. Praise choruses
   d. Benevolence
   e. None of the above

2. In 1:18, what wonderful offer did God make to His people?

Notes on Today's Bible Reading

— DAY 4 —

Today's Reading: Isaiah 3–4

Verse of the Day:

In that day the branch of the LORD shall be beautiful and glorious, and the fruit of the land shall be the pride and honor of the survivors of Israel. — Isaiah 4:2

Questions for Reflection and Discussion

1. In Isaiah's description of God's coming judgment on the nation, strong male leadership would be replaced with what?
   a. "I will make boys their princes, and infants shall rule over them."
   b. "Youth will be insolent to the elder."
   c. Weak men will declare, "You shall not make me leader of the people."
   d. "Infants are their oppressors, and women rule over them."
   e. All of the above.

2. Considering Isaiah's beautiful images of renewal in 4:2–6, when do you think God will make these things a reality? Present or future age?

Notes on Today's Bible Reading

_____

_____

_____

_____

_____

_____

_____

_____

_____

_____

_____

— DAY 5 —

Today's Reading: Isaiah 5–6

Verse of the Day:

And I heard the voice of the Lord saying, "Whom shall I send, and who will go for us?" Then I said, "Here I am! Send me." — Isaiah 6:8

Questions for Reflection and Discussion

1. What imagery did Isaiah use to illustrate the sin and ingratitude of Israel in 5:1–7?

2. What qualities of God's character and nature are revealed in 6:1–9?
    a. Holiness
    b. Sovereignty
    c. Forgiveness
    d. All of the above

Notes on Today's Bible Reading

— DAY 6 —

Today's Reading: Isaiah 7–8

Verse of the Day:

"Therefore the Lord himself will give you a sign. Behold, the virgin shall conceive and bear a son, and shall call his name Immanuel." — Isaiah 7:14

Questions for Reflection and Discussion

1. What sign was promised by God, even though King Ahaz had not asked for one (7:14–15)? How is this fulfilled in the Gospels?

2. What symbol of coming judgment did God use to describe the invading armies of the Assyrians (8:7–8)?
   a. Swarming locusts
   b. Flooding river
   c. Suffocating sandstorm
   d. None of the above

Notes on Today's Bible Reading

— DAY 7 —

Review of This Week's Readings:
Hosea 11–14; 2 Kings 15–16; Isaiah 1–8

Questions for Reflection and Discussion

1. What passage uniquely spoke to you this week?

2. What insights did you gain about God?

3. What application might this have to what is happening in the world today?

4. How would God have you apply this truth to your life?

Notes from Reflecting on This Week's Bible Readings

How do you think God feels about our current policies regarding the most vulnerable? Find out as we continue the book of Isaiah.

— DAY 1 —

Today's Reading: Isaiah 9

Verse of the Day:

The people who walked in darkness
    have seen a great light;
those who dwelt in a land of deep darkness,
    on them has light shone. — Isaiah 9:2

Questions for Reflection and Discussion

1. According to verses 1–5, where would the coming Messiah appear and minister, bringing light and joy and liberty (Matt. 4:14–16)?

2. What names are given the child to be born, the son given who will one day rule and reign (vv. 6–7)?
    a. Wonderful Counselor
    b. Mighty God
    c. Everlasting Father
    d. Prince of Peace
    e. All of the above

Notes on Today's Bible Reading

— DAY 2 —
Today's Reading: Isaiah 10

Verses of the Day:

Woe to those who decree iniquitous decrees,
    and the writers who keep writing oppression,
to turn aside the needy from justice
    and to rob the poor of my people of their right,
that widows may be their spoil,
    and that they may make the fatherless their prey! — Isaiah 10:1–2

Questions for Reflection and Discussion

1. What modern governmental practices compare to the "iniquitous decrees" and "writing oppression" that resulted in the unjust treatment of the weak (vv. 1–2)?
    a. Public policies
    b. Laws and statutes
    c. Executive orders
    d. Court rulings
    e. All of the above

2. According to verses 20–21, what words of hope did the prophet offer the children of Israel on the other side of God's judgment? And in verse 22, how does God describe the destruction He decreed?

Notes on Today's Bible Reading

_____

_____

_____

_____

_____

_____

_____

— DAY 3 —

Today's Reading: Isaiah 11–12

Verse of the Day:

They shall not hurt or destroy
　　in all my holy mountain;
for the earth shall be full of the knowledge of the LORD
　　as the waters cover the sea. — Isaiah 11:9

Questions for Reflection and Discussion

1. Who is the coming "Branch" (11:1–5), and what glorious promise did God make to the nations and to the scattered remnant of Israel and Judah (11:9–12)? See also Jeremiah 23:5–8 and 33:15–16 for more on the Branch.

2. What will God's people say in the day they joyfully "draw water from the wells of salvation" (John 7:37)?
　　a. Give thanks to the Lord and call upon His name
　　b. Make known among the nations what He has done
　　c. Proclaim that His name is exalted
　　d. Sing to the Lord for the glorious things He has done
　　e. All of the above

Notes on Today's Bible Reading

— DAY 4 —
Today's Reading: Isaiah 13

Verse of the Day:

Behold, the day of the LORD comes,
    cruel, with wrath and fierce anger,
to make the land a desolation
    and to destroy its sinners from it. — Isaiah 13:9

Questions for Reflection and Discussion

1. In verse 9, the prophet looks ahead to the "day of the Lord." Who will be punished on that day of wrath (v. 11)?

2. According to verse 17, what nation or people will carry out God's wrath on Babylon?

Notes on Today's Bible Reading

— DAY 5 —

Today's Reading: Isaiah 14

Verse of the Day:

"For the LORD will have compassion on Jacob and will again choose Israel, and will set them in their own land, and sojourners will join them and will attach themselves to the house of Jacob. — Isaiah 14:1

Questions for Reflection and Discussion

1. What welcome reversals did Isaiah prophesy for the people of Israel in verses 1–2?

2. What prideful boast of blasphemy did Lucifer/Day Star utter (vv. 13–14)?
   a. "I will ascend to heaven above the stars of God."
   b. "I will set my throne on high; I will sit on the mount of assembly."
   c. "I will ascend above the heights of the clouds; I will make myself like the Most High."
   d. All of the above.

Notes on Today's Bible Reading

— DAY 6 —

Today's Reading: Isaiah 15–16

Verse of the Day:

"[T]hen a throne will be established in steadfast love,
    and on it will sit in faithfulness
    in the tent of David
one who judges and seeks justice
    and is swift to do righteousness." — Isaiah 16:5

Questions for Reflection and Discussion

1. In God's judgment on Moab, where did he announce a throne of love and righteous judgment for all nations would be established (16:5)?

2. What major national sin on the part of the Moabites brought all the destruction and then weeping for the abundance they lost (16:6–11)?

Notes on Today's Bible Reading

— DAY 7 —
Review of This Week's Readings:
Isaiah 9–16

Questions for Reflection and Discussion

1. What passage uniquely spoke to you this week?
2. What insights did you gain about God?
3. What application might this have to what is happening in the world today?
4. How would God have you apply this truth to your life?

Notes from Reflecting on This Week's Bible Readings

How can we find peace? Find out this week as we continue the book of Isaiah.

— DAY 1 —

Today's Reading: Isaiah 17–18

Verse of the Day:

In that day man will look to his Maker, and his eyes will look on the Holy One of Israel. — Isaiah 17:7

Questions for Reflection and Discussion

1. In God's judgment on Damascus, capital of the Syrians, to whom did Isaiah say they will look in the day of judgment (17:7) rather than their pagan altars and idols (17:8)?

2. While God discouraged an alliance of Judah with the ascendant Ethiopians against the mighty Assyrians, what did Isaiah say the Ethiopian people would ultimately do according to 18:7?
   a. Go it alone against the Assyrians
   b. Team up with the Moabites and the Syrians
   c. Bring tribute to the Lord on Mount Zion
   d. None of the above

Notes on Today's Bible Reading

— DAY 2 —

Today's Reading: Isaiah 19–20

Verse of the Day:

The LORD has mingled within her a spirit of confusion,
and they will make Egypt stagger in all its deeds,
as a drunken man staggers in his vomit. — Isaiah 19:14

Questions for Reflection and Discussion

1. In God's judgment upon Egypt, whose leaders led people astray by consulting idols, sorcerers, mediums, and the necromancers, what amazing promises did Isaiah proclaim over Egypt looking forward (19:19–21)?
   a. God would send them a Savior.
   b. God would make Himself known to them.
   c. God would respond to their pleas for Him to heal them.
   d. They would acknowledge the Lord.
   e. All of the above.

2. What message was God sending to Egypt when He instructed Isaiah to go about naked and barefoot for three years as a sign (20:1–4)? What effect did this have on those who put their trust in Egypt (vv. 5–6)?

Notes on Today's Bible Reading

— DAY 3 —

Today's Reading: Isaiah 21–22

Verses of the Day:

He has taken away the covering of Judah.
In that day you looked to the weapons of the House of the Forest, and you saw that the breaches of the city of David were many. You collected the waters of the lower pool, and you counted the houses of Jerusalem, and you broke down the houses to fortify the wall. You made a reservoir between the two walls for the water of the old pool. But you did not look to him who did it, or see him who planned it long ago. — Isaiah 22:8–11

Questions for Reflection and Discussion

1. According to Isaiah 21:6–7, what did the watchman, posted day and night, see and hear?

2. When Isaiah foresaw the destruction of Jerusalem, what actions did the people take to protect themselves (22:8–11)? What action was the Lord looking for (v. 12)?

Notes on Today's Bible Reading

_____

_____

_____

_____

_____

_____

_____

_____

_____

_____

— DAY 4 —
Today's Reading: Isaiah 23

Verse of the Day:

At the end of seventy years, the Lord will visit Tyre, and she will return to her wages and will prostitute herself with all the kingdoms of the world on the face of the earth. — Isaiah 23:17

Questions for Reflection and Discussion

1. In God's pronouncement of judgment upon Tyre, what was the principal sin according to verse 9?

2. How long would Tyre experience God's judgment (v. 17), and what would happen after Tyre returned to her trade and her earnings (v. 18)?

Notes on Today's Bible Reading

— DAY 5 —

Today's Reading: Isaiah 24–25

Verse of the Day:

Terror and the pit and the snare
    are upon you, O inhabitant of the earth! — Isaiah 24:17

Questions for Reflection and Discussion

1. Who would be affected by the devastation God announced in 24:1–3?
   a. Priest and people
   b. Slave and master
   c. Buyer and seller
   d. Lender and borrower
   e. All of the above

2. What will God be like for the poor and needy according to 25:4?

Notes on Today's Bible Reading

— DAY 6 —

Today's Reading: Isaiah 26–27

Verse of the Day:

"You keep him in perfect peace,
    whose mind is stayed on you,
    because he trusts in you." — Isaiah 26:3

Questions for Reflection and Discussion

1. Who is the person God keeps in perfect peace according to 26:3?

2. To what creature did Isaiah compare God's defeat of evil in 27:1?

Notes on Today's Bible Reading

— DAY 7 —
Review of This Week's Readings:
Isaiah 17–27

Questions for Reflection and Discussion

1. What passage uniquely spoke to you this week?

2. What insights did you gain about God?

3. What application might this have to what is happening in the world today?

4. How would God have you apply this truth to your life?

Notes from Reflecting on This Week's Bible Readings

What governing functions does God perfectly provide? Find out this week as we continue studying the book of Isaiah.

— DAY 1 —

Today's Reading: Isaiah 28

Verse of the Day:

[T]herefore thus says the Lord God,
"Behold, I am the one who has laid as a foundation in Zion,
    a stone, a tested stone,
a precious cornerstone, of a sure foundation:
    'Whoever believes will not be in haste.'" — Isaiah 28:16

Questions for Reflection and Discussion

1. What will the Lord of Hosts be like to the remnant of His people (vv. 5–6)?
   a. Crown of glory
   b. Diadem of beauty
   c. Spirit of justice
   d. Strength
   e. All of the above

2. According to the apostle Peter, to whom does the prophecy in Isaiah 28:16 refer (1 Pet. 2:6–7)?

Notes on Today's Bible Reading

— DAY 2 —
Today's Reading: Isaiah 29

Verses of the Day:

And the Lord said:
"Because this people draw near with their mouth
    and honor me with their lips,
    while their hearts are far from me,
and their fear of me is a commandment taught by men,
therefore, behold, I will again
    do wonderful things with this people,
    with wonder upon wonder;
and the wisdom of their wise men shall perish,
    and the discernment of their discerning men shall be
    hidden." — Isaiah 29:13–14

Questions for Reflection and Discussion

1. What described the people's hypocritical condition prior to God's judgment upon them (v. 13)? See also Jesus's use of this scripture in Matthew 15:8–9.
   a. Come near to God with their mouths
   b. Honor God with their lips
   c. Hearts are far from God
   d. Worship is made up from man-made rules
   e. All of the above

2. When Messiah comes, what are some of the miraculous signs Isaiah predicted will take place (vv. 18–19; compare with Matt. 11:4)?

Notes on Today's Bible Reading

— DAY 3 —

Today's Reading: Isaiah 30–31

Verses of the Day:

For they are a rebellious people,
 lying children,
children unwilling to hear
 the instruction of the LORD;
who say to the seers, "Do not see,"
 and to the prophets, "Do not prophesy to us what is right;
speak to us smooth things,
 prophesy illusions,
leave the way, turn aside from the path,
 let us hear no more about the Holy One of Israel."

— Isaiah 30:9–11

Questions for Reflection and Discussion

1. In a time of trouble, whose help did the children of Israel seek (30:2), and what did God's people say to His messengers—the seers and prophets (vv. 9–11)?

2. Despite the rebellion of God's people and the consequences, what longing did God express in verse 18? What promises did He reveal for a time to come (vv. 19–22)?

Notes on Today's Bible Reading

— DAY 4 —

Today's Reading: Isaiah 32

Verse of the Day:

Behold, a king will reign in righteousness,
and princes will rule in justice. — Isaiah 32:1

Questions for Reflection and Discussion

1. According to Isaiah 32:1–2, what are rulers like who lead in righteousness and justice?
    a. "Hiding place from the wind"
    b. "Shelter from the storm"
    c. "Streams of water in a dry place"
    d. "Shade of a great rock in a weary land"
    e. All of the above

2. What change agent will spark the switch from judgment to blessing (v. 15)?

Notes on Today's Bible Reading

— DAY 5 —

Today's Reading: Isaiah 33

Verse of the Day:

For the LORD is our judge; the LORD is our lawgiver;
    the LORD is our king; he will save us." — Isaiah 33:22

Questions for Reflection and Discussion

1. In verse 15, what are some of the marks of the righteous?

2. The Lord functions in what roles that correspond to branches of American government (v. 22)?
    a. Judge (Judicial)
    b. Lawgiver (Legislative)
    c. King (Executive)
    d. All of the above

Notes on Today's Bible Reading

— DAY 6 —

Today's Reading: Isaiah 34–35

Verse of the Day:

Say to those who have an anxious heart,
    "Be strong; fear not!
Behold, your God
    will come with vengeance,
with the recompense of God.
    He will come and save you." — Isaiah 35:4

Questions for Reflection and Discussion

1. According to 34:5–8, what figurative weapon will the Lord wield in retribution on behalf of Zion?

2. According to 35:5–10, what are some of the miraculous signs that will be common in the coming kingdom of God?

Notes on Today's Bible Reading

— DAY 7 —
Review of This Week's Readings:
Isaiah 28–35

Questions for Reflection and Discussion

1. What passage uniquely spoke to you this week?

2. What insights did you gain about God?

3. What application might this have to what is happening in the world today?

4. How would God have you apply this truth to your life?

Notes from Reflecting on This Week's Bible Readings

_____

_____

_____

_____

_____

_____

_____

_____

_____

_____

_____

_____

_____

_____

_____

Week 51

What three qualities does God require? Find out as we read the book of Micah.

For an introduction to Micah, see appendix 1, page 411.

— DAY 1 —

Today's Reading: Micah 1–2

Verse of the Day:

Hear, you peoples, all of you;
      pay attention, O earth, and all that is in it,
and let the Lord God be a witness against you,
      the Lord from his holy temple. — Micah 1:2

Questions for Reflection and Discussion

1. Why was God's judgment coming on His people according to 1:5?

2. Despite God's judgment on His people, what would God do for them in the future according to 2:12–13?

Notes on Today's Bible Reading

— DAY 2 —

Today's Reading: Micah 3–5

Verse of the Day:

But you, O Bethlehem Ephrathah,
    who are too little to be among the clans of Judah,
from you shall come forth for me
    one who is to be ruler in Israel,
whose coming forth is from of old,
    from ancient days. — Micah 5:2

Questions for Reflection and Discussion

1. According to Micah 3, what marked the leadership of the rulers of the house of Jacob and house of Israel?
    a. Executed justice
    b. Established righteousness
    c. Built Zion on respect for life
    d. Trusted the Lord to protect them because of their godliness
    e. None of the above

2. In Micah 5:2–5, the prophet predicts the coming of Israel's King (Messiah) who will shepherd His flock and be their peace more than seven hundred years before His actual birth. Where does Micah tell us He will be born? Compare these verses with Matthew 2:1–6.

Notes on Today's Bible Reading

— DAY 3 —

Today's Reading: Micah 6–7

Verse of the Day:

He has told you, O man, what is good;
>   and what does the Lord require of you
but to do justice, and to love kindness,
>   and to walk humbly with your God? — Micah 6:8

Questions for Reflection and Discussion

1. According to Micah, what does the Lord require (6:8)?
   a. Do justice
   b. Love kindness/mercy
   c. Walk humbly with your God
   d. All of the above

2. In the conclusion of his prophecy, what did Micah affirm about God, and what was the basis of his confidence that God would act this way toward His people (7:18–20)?

Notes on Today's Bible Reading

— DAY 4 —

Today's Reading: 2 Kings 17

Verse of the Day:

And this occurred because the people of Israel had sinned against the LORD their God, who had brought them up out of the land of Egypt from under the hand of Pharaoh king of Egypt, and had feared other gods. — 2 Kings 17:7

Questions for Reflection and Discussion

1. What caused Israel's downfall, which resulted in the Assyrians invading and deporting them (17:7–18)?

2. The king of Assyria repopulated Samaria with exiles from other conquered nations who did not worship the Lord, and the new inhabitants were plagued by lions (v. 25). What was the pagan king's surprising response (vv. 27–28)?

Notes on Today's Bible Reading

— DAY 5 —

Today's Reading: 2 Kings 18

Verse of the Day:

He trusted in the LORD, the God of Israel, so that there was none like him among all the kings of Judah after him, nor among those who were before him. — 2 Kings 18:5

Questions for Reflection and Discussion

1. What drastic measures did young King Hezekiah undertake in verses 3–6, signaling a dramatic return to the Lord, that resulted in the positive affirmation in verse 7: "And the Lord was with him; wherever he went out, he prospered"?
    a. Removed the high places
    b. Broke the pagan pillars
    c. Cut down the Asherah
    d. Broke into pieces the bronze serpent
    e. All of the above

2. What was the response of the people to the scare tactics of Sennacherib, king of Assyria, who sent his supreme commander, chief officer, and his field commander with a large army to threaten King Hezekiah (vv. 26–36)?

Notes on Today's Bible Reading

— DAY 6 —

Today's Reading: 2 Kings 19

Verse of the Day:

And Hezekiah prayed before the LORD and said: "O LORD, the God of Israel, enthroned above the cherubim, you are the God, you alone, of all the kingdoms of the earth; you have made heaven and earth." — 2 Kings 19:15

Questions for Reflection and Discussion

1. What was King Hezekiah's immediate response to the threatening taunts of the Assyrian commander and his officials? Where did Hezekiah send the palace administrator, the secretary, and the leading priests (vv. 1–2)?

2. When Hezekiah spread out the Assyrian's letter before the Lord, what did he request from God (vv. 14–19)?
   a. That He would hear the words Sennacherib, who was sent to mock the living God
   b. That He would open His eyes and see
   c. That He would save them and that all the kingdoms of the earth may know that He alone is God
   d. All of the above

Notes on Today's Bible Reading

— DAY 7 —
Review of This Week's Readings:
Micah 1–7; 2 Kings 17–19

Questions for Reflection and Discussion

1. What passage uniquely spoke to you this week?

2. What insights did you gain about God?

3. What application might this have to what is happening in the world today?

4. How would God have you apply this truth to your life?

Notes from Reflecting on This Week's Bible Readings

_____

_____

_____

_____

_____

_____

_____

_____

_____

_____

_____

_____

_____

_____

What are some of the key character qualities of the coming Messiah? Find out as we continue reading the prophecy of Isaiah.

— DAY 1 —

Today's Reading: 2 Kings 20

Verse of the Day:

"Turn back, and say to Hezekiah the leader of my people, Thus says the LORD, the God of David your father: I have heard your prayer; I have seen your tears. Behold, I will heal you. On the third day you shall go up to the house of the LORD." — 2 Kings 20:5

Questions for Reflection and Discussion

1. When the prophet Isaiah told Hezekiah he would die from his illness, Hezekiah wept bitterly and desperately prayed for God to spare his life. What was God's response (vv. 4–6)?

2. What was Isaiah's message to Hezekiah after learning that Hezekiah had revealed all the treasures of his kingdom to envoys from Babylon (vv. 16–18)?

Notes on Today's Bible Reading

_____

_____

_____

_____

_____

_____

_____

_____

— DAY 2 —

Today's Reading: Isaiah 36

Verse of the Day:

In the fourteenth year of King Hezekiah, Sennacherib king of Assyria came up against all the fortified cities of Judah and took them. — Isaiah 36:1

Questions for Reflection and Discussion

1. What key question did the Assyrians pose to Hezekiah's representatives (vv. 4–5)?

2. Speaking in Hebrew, Rabshakeh, the Assyrian military leader, sought to strike fear in the hearts of the people of Judah and shatter their faith. By whose authority did the Rabshakeh claim to speak (v. 10)?

Notes on Today's Bible Reading

— DAY 3 —

Today's Reading: Isaiah 37

Verses of the Day:

Hezekiah received the letter from the hand of the messengers, and read it; and Hezekiah went up to the house of the Lord, and spread it before the Lord. And Hezekiah prayed to the Lord. — Isaiah 37:14–15

Questions for Reflection and Discussion

1. After Hezekiah learned of Assyria's plan to conquer Judah, what was Hezekiah's bold profession of faith declared through his prayer in the temple (vv. 15–19)? And what was his petition (v. 20)?

2. Because Hezekiah prayed to God concerning the king of Assyria (v. 21), God promised to defend Jerusalem. What miraculous action did God take to fulfill His promise (vv. 36–38)?

Notes on Today's Bible Reading

— DAY 4 —

Today's Reading: Isaiah 38–39

Verses of the Day:

"This shall be the sign to you from the Lord, that the Lord will do this thing that he has promised: Behold, I will make the shadow cast by the declining sun on the dial of Ahaz turn back ten steps." So the sun turned back on the dial the ten steps by which it had declined. — Isaiah 38:7–8

Questions for Reflection and Discussion

1. What miraculous sign did God give to Hezekiah to assure him of his healing (38:7–8)?

2. What was Hezekiah's response to Isaiah's prophecy concerning the future defeat and exile of Judah, including some of his own sons who would go into captivity (39:5–8)?

Notes on Today's Bible Reading

— DAY 5 —

Today's Reading: Isaiah 40

Verse of the Day:

[B]ut they who wait for the Lord shall renew their strength;
  they shall mount up with wings like eagles;
they shall run and not be weary;
  they shall walk and not faint. — Isaiah 40:31

Questions for Reflection and Discussion

1. The fulfillment of Isaiah 40:3–5 can be found in the Gospels (Luke 3:4–6) with the mission of John the Baptist and ministry of the Messiah, who would tend His flock like a Shepherd and carry His lambs close to His heart. How could God's people be sure these promises would be fulfilled (Isa. 40:8)?

2. What promises are given to those who wait in dependence on the Lord (40:31)?
 a. Renew their strength
 b. Soar on wings like eagles
 c. Run and not be weary
 d. Walk and not faint
 e. All of the above

Notes on Today's Bible Reading

_____

_____

_____

_____

_____

_____

_____

_____

_____

_____

_____

— DAY 6 —
Today's Reading: Isaiah 41

Verse of the Day:

[F]ear not, for I am with you;
    be not dismayed, for I am your God;
I will strengthen you, I will help you,
    I will uphold you with my righteous right hand. — Isaiah 41:10

Questions for Reflection and Discussion

1. What words of comfort did God announce to His people through Isaiah (vv. 10–14)?
   a. "I am with you; be not dismayed, for I am your God."
   b. "I will strengthen you, I will help you."
   c. "I will uphold you with my righteous right hand."
   d. All of the above.

2. What primary challenge did the Lord place before the idols of Israel's enemies (vv. 21–24)?

Notes on Today's Bible Reading

— DAY 7 —

Review of This Week's Readings:
2 Kings 20; Isaiah 36–41

Questions for Reflection and Discussion

1. What passage uniquely spoke to you this week?

2. What insights did you gain about God?

3. What application might this have to what is happening in the world today?

4. How would God have you apply this truth to your life?

Notes from Reflecting on This Week's Bible Readings

What world ruler was announced more than 150 years before he arrived to advocate for Judah? Find out this week as we continue through Isaiah.

— DAY 1 —

Today's Reading: Isaiah 42–43

Verse of the Day:

"Behold my servant, whom I uphold,
    my chosen, in whom my soul delights;
I have put my Spirit upon him;
    he will bring forth justice to the nations." — Isaiah 42:1

Questions for Reflection and Discussion

1. Who is the Servant described in 42:1–4 (Matt. 12:15–21)?
2. Is the Lord willing to share His glory with rivals (Isa. 42:8)?

Notes on Today's Bible Reading

— DAY 2 —

Today's Reading: Isaiah 44

Verse of the Day:

Thus says the LORD, the King of Israel
 and his Redeemer, the LORD of hosts:
"I am the first and I am the last;
 besides me there is no god." — Isaiah 44:6

Questions for Reflection and Discussion

1. What images did Isaiah use to illustrate the outpouring of the Holy Spirit (vv. 3–4)?

2. After Isaiah humorously described at length the process of constructing an idol, what is the conclusion reached in verses 18–20 about the idol maker who becomes an idol worshipper?

Notes on Today's Bible Reading

— DAY 3 —

Today's Reading: Isaiah 45

Verse of the Day:

"Turn to me and be saved, all the ends of the earth! For I am God, and there is no other." — Isaiah 45:22

Questions for Reflection and Discussion

1. Why would God raise the Persian ruler Cyrus to prominence (vv. 5–7)?

2. What would Cyrus do for God's people that was beyond their expectation (vv. 11–13)?

Notes on Today's Bible Reading

— DAY 4 —

Today's Reading: Isaiah 46–47

Verse of the Day:

"To whom will you liken me and make me equal, and compare me, that we may be alike?" — Isaiah 46:5

Questions for Reflection and Discussion

1. What is God's role in what happens in the future (46:8–11)?
   a. He is watching it unfold like the rest of us.
   b. He is crossing His fingers and hoping for the best.
   c. He declares the end from the beginning and will bring it to pass.
   d. None of the above.

2. In what did Babylon trust, and what would be the result (47:10–11)?

Notes on Today's Bible Reading

— DAY 5 —

Today's Reading: Isaiah 48

Verse of the Day:

"The former things I declared of old; they went out from my mouth, and I announced them; then suddenly I did them, and they came to pass." — Isaiah 48:3

Questions for Reflection and Discussion

1. What ability did the Lord tout as a difference between Himself and worthless idols (vv. 3–5)?

2. What was God's reason for delaying His wrath against Judah (v. 9)?

Notes on Today's Bible Reading

— DAY 6 —

Today's Reading: Isaiah 49

Verse of the Day:

"Sing for joy, O heavens, and exult, O earth;
  break forth, O mountains, into singing!
For the Lord has comforted his people
  and will have compassion on his afflicted." — Isaiah 49:13

Questions for Reflection and Discussion

1. Besides sending Messiah to bring Israel back to the Lord, what was God's greater purpose for Him (v. 6)?
   a. Judge of the wicked
   b. Miracle worker
   c. Light to the nations
   d. None of the above

2. What was the reply the Lord gave to the claim that He had forgotten Zion (vv. 14–19)?

Notes on Today's Bible Reading

— DAY 7 —
Review of This Week's Readings:
Isaiah 42–49

Questions for Reflection and Discussion

1. What passage uniquely spoke to you this week?

2. What insights did you gain about God?

3. What application might this have to what is happening in the world today?

4. How would God have you apply this truth to your life?

In our chronologically prioritized reading, the following books of the Bible are covered in the order they are introduced:

- Genesis
- Job
- Exodus
- Leviticus
- Numbers
- Deuteronomy
- Joshua
- Judges
- Ruth

- 1 Samuel
- 2 Samuel
- 1 Chronicles
- Psalms
- 1 Kings
- Proverbs
- Song of Solomon
- 2 Chronicles

- Ecclesiastes
- 2 Kings
- Joel
- Amos
- Jonah
- Hosea
- Isaiah
- Micah

Genesis

Moses wrote Genesis as the first of five books of the Bible we call the Torah. Genesis provides a brief history of God's creation and broad story of humanity then zeroes in on the history of God's special relationship with those forefathers—their origins, their journeys, and their covenants with Him. Because the events contained in the rest of the Torah are responses to the promises of God found in Genesis, such a history not only provided encouragement and inspiration to these former slaves seeking freedom and but firmly established their identity as God's chosen people Israel in their promised land. Consequently, the book of Genesis can be divided into two main sections: Primitive History and Patriarchal History.

- Part 1 of Genesis presents Primitive History and records: (1) the creation (chaps. 1–2); (2) the fall (3–5); (3) the flood (6–9); and (4) the dispersion from Babel (10–11).
- Part 2 of Genesis traces Patriarchal History and records the lives of four principle people: (1) Abraham (chaps. 12–25:8); (2) Isaac (21:1–35:29); (3) Jacob (25:21–50:14); and (4) Joseph (30:22–50:26).

The great questions of life are answered in Genesis: (1) Where did I come from? (God created us, 1:1); (2) Why am I here? (we are here to have a relationship with God based on faith, 15:6) (3) Where am I going? (we have a destination after death, 25:8).

Genesis is a book of firsts. The first man and woman, the first marriage, the first sin, the first children, the first sacrifices, the first murder, and so on. And we're also introduced to concepts such as self-government, family government, and civil government.

Yet we not only learn about the first sin and its destructive effects on humanity; we also get a glimpse of God's gracious plan to atone for that sin through the seed of a woman, a future Son of Abraham, and a ruler from the tribe of Judah (3:15; 22:18; 49:10). While Satan the serpent will bruise His heel, this promised Savior will crush the serpent's head!

Job

The author of the book of Job is unknown, but most likely an eyewitness recorded the detailed and lengthy conversations found in the book, which is categorized as Wisdom literature because it reflects on how to make sense of suffering. We don't know much about Job personally other than he was a wealthy landowner, husband of one wife, and father of a large family. He was stripped of everything, his faith was severely tested, and yet he survived by the grace of God and became one of the best-known biblical heroes. We read that Job lived in the land of Uz (1:1), but its location is unknown.

According to 42:16, Job lived an additional 140 years after his tragedies occurred, perhaps to around 210 years total. His long life span generally corresponds to that of Terah (Abraham's father), Abraham, Isaac, and Jacob. Also Job's wealth was measured in livestock (1:3; 42:12), as was Abraham's (Gen. 12:16). Like the patriarchs, Job used God's unique title "El Shaddai" (God Almighty). The book of Job does not mention the Mosaic law; indeed, Job's daughters were equal heirs with his sons, and Job himself, though not a priest, offered sacrifices—things not possible under the Law (Lev. 4:10; Num. 27:8). Consequently, Job probably lived during the time of the patriarchs, approximately 2100 to 1900 BC.

The prologue gives us an inside look into God's throne room and how Satan requested and God allowed him to afflict Job. From that prologue we learn: (1) Satan cannot bring physical or financial destruction upon us unless God allows it. (2) God has power over what Satan can and cannot do. (3) Not all suffering is the result of sin. Then through a series of dialogues and monologues arranged in a pattern of threes, human wisdom attempts to explain the unexplainable, until finally God Himself speaks. The final chapters of Job record God's masterful defense of His sovereign majesty and eternal transcendence above creation—in contrast with Job's frailty as a mere man: "Where were you when I laid the foundation of the earth? Tell me, if you have understanding" (Job 38:4).

At the end of the day, God does not supply a clear answer regarding Job's suffering, but He does graciously restore Job's wealth and family so that his later state is greater than his former.

Job's plight of undeserved suffering compels us to ask the age-old question, Why do bad things happen to good people? The answer given to Job may or may not satisfy the reader. God allows pain and suffering sometimes for reasons beyond our understanding, but we know that God is sovereign; He loves us, and for those who love him, He works all things, even our suffering, together for good and for His glory. So trust God in your trials. Let him refine you in that refiners fire until your character comes forth as gold, and you reflect his glory.

Exodus

Moses wrote the book of Exodus between 1440 and 1400 BC. The title "Exodus" comes from the Greek Septuagint and describes the primary event found in the book: the deliverance from slavery and "exodus" or departure of God's chosen people out of Egypt by the hand of Yahweh—the God of their forefathers—and led by his servant Moses. The exodus of the Israelites from Egypt marked the end of a period of oppression and bondage for Abraham's descendants (Gen. 15:13) and the beginning of the fulfillment of the covenant promise to Abraham that his descendants would not only live in the promised land but would also multiply and become a great nation (Gen. 12:1–3, 7).

Exodus begins where Genesis leaves off. It traces the events from the time Israel entered Egypt as guests of Joseph, second only to Pharaoh in Egypt, until they were eventually delivered from the cruel bondage of slavery by "a new king . . . who did not know Joseph" (Exod. 1:8).

The first section tells us how God miraculously and dramatically freed His people from bondage to Pharaoh under the leadership of Moses. It describes the oppression of the Jews under the cruel Pharaoh, the rise of Moses as their deliverer, the plagues God brought upon Egypt for the refusal of Pharaoh to submit to Him, and the departure from Egypt. God's sovereign and powerful hand is seen in the plagues—ending with the plague of death of the firstborn and the institution of the first Passover—the deliverance of the Israelites, the parting of the Red Sea, and the destruction of the Egyptian army.

The middle section of Exodus is about how God then established Israel as a theocratic nation under His covenant on Mount Sinai. This section tells of their time with Yahweh God in the wilderness and at Mount Sinai and God's miraculous provision, the establishment of His covenant, and the giving of His law. But even though He gave them bread from heaven, sweet water from bitter, water from a rock, victory over those who would destroy them, His Law written on tablets of stone by His own hand, and His presence to guide them in the form of pillars of fire and cloud, the people continually grumbled and rebelled against Him.

The last third of the book describes in detail the construction of the ark of the covenant and the plan for the tabernacle with its various sacrifices, altars, furniture, ceremonies, and forms of worship.

Throughout Exodus are several prophetic types of Christ: The numerous sacrifices required of the Israelites were a picture of the ultimate sacrifice, the Passover Lamb of God,

Jesus Christ. The night of the last plague on Egypt, an unblemished lamb was killed and its blood applied to the doorposts of the houses of God's people, protecting them from the angel of death. This foreshadowed Jesus, the Lamb of God "without blemish or spot" (1 Pet. 1:19), whose blood applied to us ensures eternal life. Among the symbolic presentations of Christ in the book of Exodus is the story of the water from the rock (17:1–7). Just as Moses struck the rock to provide life-giving water for the people to drink, so did God strike the Rock of our salvation, crucifying Him for our sin, and from the Rock came the gift of living water (John 4:10). The provision of manna in the wilderness is a perfect picture of Christ, the Bread of life (John 6:48), provided by God to give us life.

The overall theme of Exodus is redemption—how God delivered the Israelites and made them His covenant people under the leadership of Moses.

Leviticus

The word *Leviticus* is a Latin title that points back to the tribe of Levi, whose members were set aside by the Lord to be His priests and worship leaders, and they are a big part of this book. Moses wrote this third book of the Law at or near Mount Sinai, where the Israelites camped for some time in the 1440s BC, and it is a departure from the mostly narrative story we've been accustomed to in Genesis and Exodus. In Leviticus, we have mostly a collection of rituals, rules, and guidelines for godly living. Yet within these highly detailed directives we discover not only the holiness of God, but we learn how sin separates and devastates our relationship with our Creator and requires atonement.

Here's a brief summary of the sections:

- Chapters 1–7 outline the offerings required of both laypeople and the priesthood.
- Chapters 8–10 describe the consecration of Aaron and his sons to the priesthood.
- Chapters 11–15 are the prescriptions for various types of uncleanness.
- Chapter 16 describes the Day of Atonement when an annual sacrifice is made for the cumulative sin of the people.
- Chapters 17–27 contain God's guidelines to His people for practical holiness so that they can live separate, distinct, God-honoring lives in contrast to the peoples around them.

The primary theme of Leviticus is holiness. God's call to holiness in His people is based on His own character and nature as holy. Like two sides of one coin, the corresponding theme is that of atonement. To maintain holiness before God, it can only be attained through a proper atonement. Consequently the purpose of Leviticus is to provide instruction and laws to guide a sinful, yet redeemed people in the pursuit of holiness in their relationship with a holy God.

Obviously, all of the sacrifices, rituals, and festivals foreshadow the ultimate sacrifice Christ made on the cross. So on this side of the cross, we can praise the Lord that because of Jesus's death on our behalf as a substitute we no longer have to offer animal sacrifices. His once-for-all sacrifice enables us to stand before a holy God without fear because He sees in us the applied righteousness of Christ.

But the book of Leviticus calls us as believers to live out practically what we are positionally in Christ. To be holy as God is holy.

Numbers

The book of Numbers is the fourth book Moses wrote. In fact, it specifically mentions Moses recording events by the Lord's commands (Num. 33:2; 36:13). So he's obviously the author, as he is of all five books of the Law, the Torah. The name "Numbers" is a translation of the title *Arithmoi*, from the Greek Septuagint, from which we get our "arithmetic." The reason becomes obvious because the book contains census figures, population counts, and numerical data regarding the tribes and the priestly line of Levi. The Hebrew name comes from the first sentence of the book, which includes "in the wilderness." Actually, that Hebrew title provides a more accurate description of the book's content, which is basically Moses's travelogue of the Israelites as they wander through the wilderness for nearly forty years. And just like a family road trip, there was a lot of complaining and are-we-there-yet moments.

The events of Numbers begin in the second year after the Israelites departed Egypt, as they camped at Mount Sinai around 1444 BC (1:1). And this book ends thirty-eight years later "in the plains of Moab by the Jordan at Jericho" (36:13) in 1406 BC. So Numbers essentially bridges the gap between the Israelites receiving the Law (in Exodus and Leviticus) and preparing them to enter the promised land (in Deuteronomy and Joshua).

What was only an eleven-day journey from Mount Sinai to the edge of the promised land, became a forty-year journey of judgment on that generation because of their disbelief and disobedience in Numbers 14. The report of the spies and the mutiny of the people are the pivotal moment of the book. God's judgment was everyone in that generation was condemned to die in the wilderness, with the exception of Caleb and Joshua, who believed God. So the first twenty-five chapters focus on the generation that came out of Egypt and died on the journey, while the final chapters focus on the next generation, which entered the promised land.

Numbers takes us on a long and winding path through a desert of sometimes numbing detail. The book records census results for all twelve tribes not once but twice; it documents priestly instructions for handling the ark of the covenant and the tabernacle; and it even spells out the placement of the tribes when they camped. But through it all, we get glimpses of God's unfailing direction of and presence with the nation, guiding them with the pillar of fire by night and cloud by day and providing them with manna and water to sustain them.

More than an accounting ledger and history lesson, the book of Numbers continues the theme of God's holiness from Leviticus and reveals the tough truth that God does not tolerate disbelief and disobedience, grumbling and complaining about his providence. At the same time He graciously and faithfully guides and provides. He keeps His promises. Even when we are unfaithful, God proves Himself faithful.

Deuteronomy

The English title "Deuteronomy" comes from the Septuagint and literally means "second law." The Hebrew title is *Dĕbārim*, which means "the words." These are the words that Moses spoke to all Israel. So both titles are appropriate. Deuteronomy is basically a collection of Moses's sermons to Israel, restating and interpreting God's law for a new generation.

Moses wrote this fifth book around 1406 BC at the conclusion of the forty years of wilderness wandering. At the time, the people were camped on the east side of the Jordan River, on the plains of Moab, across from the city of Jericho (Deut. 1:1; 29:1). Moses called on this new generation of Israelites to renew the covenant

with Yahweh as preparation for conquering and settling the promised land. His sermons were given across a forty-day period prior to them mourning Moses's death then entering the land.

Here is a brief summary of the sections:

- Chapters 1–4 recap their forty-year journey from Egypt to their current location across the Jordan. Moses called them to obey the covenant first established at Sinai and to be faithful to God, who was faithful to them on the journey.
- Chapters 5–26 are a restating and interpretation of the Law, the contents of the covenant. Moses restated the Ten Commandments and the laws concerning sacrifices and specials days and gave the rest of the laws to the new generation.
- Chapters 27–30 are dominated by the theme of blessing and cursing. Moses stated the consequences of the covenant for the new generation: a blessing if they remain faithful and obedient but a curse if they do not. Even the exile was predicted.
- Chapters 31–34 bring us to the conclusion. Moses makes a final appeal to the people, commissions Joshua as his replacement, records a song of worship and warning, and gives a final blessing to each of the tribes of Israel. The final chapter relates the circumstances of Moses' death and concludes with a brief obituary for this great prophet of God.

Speaking of prophets, Moses predicts another prophet will come: the Prophet who is the Messiah (18:15–18). Like Moses, He would hear from God, speak His words, and lead His people (John 6:14; 7:40). Interestingly, Jesus quoted from Deuteronomy more than any other book of the Pentateuch—in fact more than any other Old Testament book except the Psalms.

One of the key passages in Deuteronomy is what is called *Shema*, the basic confession of faith in Judaism even today: "Hear, O Israel: The LORD our God, the LORD is one. You shall love the LORD your God with all your heart and with all your soul and with all your might" (6:4–5). This is the great commandment Jesus quoted. While God repeatedly invited His people to love Him, He also proclaimed His love for them in Deuteronomy. The Lord said it was His love for them that motivated Him to bring Israel out of Egypt with a mighty hand and make them his own (7:7–9). What a wonderful thing to be the object of God's love! But when they enjoyed the fruit of the promised land, there was a temptation to forget the Lord who loved them so much. Moses encouraged them again and again to remember (e.g., chap. 8).

He also urged them to remain loyal and obey the Lord. Unlike the unconditional covenant God made with Abraham, the covenant between Yahweh and Israel was conditional. God would keep His promise to bless the nation if the people remained faithful. Moses concluded his message on the covenant with this challenge: "I have set before you life and death, blessing and curse. Therefore choose life, that you and your offspring may live, loving the LORD your God, obeying his voice and by holding fast to him, for he is your life and length of days" (30:19–20).

Joshua

The book of Joshua continues the story of the Israelites after their exodus from Egypt, and wilderness wanderings, with the focus on taking the promised land. In fact, the purpose of the book of Joshua is to tell us how to be successful in taking possession of God's promise. And that begins and ends with trusting and obeying God

and His word: "Only be strong and very courageous, being careful to do according to all the law that Moses my servant commanded you. Do not turn from it to the right hand or to the left, that you may have good success wherever you go" (Josh. 1:7).

The name *Joshua* means "Yahweh saves or delivers," which is an appropriate name for the man who was God's choice to lead Israel to victory over their enemies and the conquest of Canaan. With the passing of Moses and the rise of Joshua to leadership, there was a new direction. We move from Moses and his five Law books to Joshua's book of history that recounts God's faithfulness in giving Israel the promised land.

Most Old Testament scholars believe Joshua recorded or directed a scribe to record the vast majority of the book. In fact, early chapters include firsthand accounts with personal pronouns (e.g., 5:1, 6). Plus, the book is full of military strategy, tactics, and details that God's general, Joshua, obviously directed. Added to this the fact that 24:26 refers to Joshua writing down the law of God. It stands to reason if Joshua could copy at least Deuteronomy, if not the entire Torah, he could have written most of the book that bears his name as well. Obviously, after Joshua's death, the high priests Eleazar or Phinehas may have added some of the materials about events after the conquest (15:13–19; 19:47; 24:29–33) and wrapped up the book.

The events of the book of Joshua span about twenty-five to thirty years, starting soon after the death of Moses (1:1) around 1406 BC. It begins with the Lord commissioning Joshua as the new leader with the nation of Israel poised on the banks of the Jordan River, across from Jericho. Once the conquest commenced, it took about seven years to break the main force's resistance. In the middle of that, the covenant with Yahweh was renewed for a new generation at Shechem, then the land was apportioned, and mop-up operations continued through the end of the book. Joshua's final address and subsequent death came almost thirty years after combat operations began.

Four words summarize the division of the book of Joshua's twenty-four chapters: *cross, take, divide,* and *serve*:

- Chapters 1–5: "*Cross* the Jordan into the land I have given you."
- Chapters 6–12: "*Take* the land I have given you."
- Chapters 13–21: "*Divide* the land I have given you."
- Chapters 22–24: "*Serve* the Lord in the land I have given you."

Obviously, Joshua is a pivotal Old Testament book, and the man Joshua points to Jesus. As Moses was a type of Jesus, who is the ultimate lawgiver, in many ways, his protégé Joshua is a type of Jesus, who is the ultimate deliverer. In fact, Joshua and Jesus bear the same Hebrew name, which means "Yahweh saves." Just as Joshua delivered the people from their enemies, in the greater sense, Jesus delivers us from sin and Satan.

Joshua is a prime example of the benefits of a having a faithful mentor. Moses discipled him, and Joshua learned to talk and walk with God in a personal way. He learned how to obey and the negatives of disobedience through Moses's example. Mentoring is far more than the words that are spoken—a mentor's entire life is on display. Moses provided that for Joshua. He certainly set Joshua up for success. The great tragedy of Joshua's life is that he apparently did not provide the same for a successor, and the whole nation of Israel suffered in the succeeding

generations; they drifted away from the Lord without a strong leader after Joshua passed.

At the same time, Joshua gives us a perfect road map for successful Christian living. It all comes back to trusting and obeying the word of God. To do that we've got to be strong and courageous although this runs counter to the culture. At the end of the book, Joshua presents loyalty to the Lord as a choice we must make, a stand we must take. May we declare with Joshua, "As for me and for my house, we will serve the Lord" (24:15).

Judges

Rabbinic tradition names the prophetic priest Samuel, who was also the final judge, as the author of the book of Judges. It functions as the sequel to the historical book of Joshua, linked by parallel accounts of Joshua's death (Josh. 24:29–31; Judg. 2:6–9). Events within Judges span the geographical breadth of the nation, occurring in a variety of tribes, cities, and battlefields. Scholars believe some of the judges may have ruled simultaneously in separate geographical regions of Israel. Consequently it's difficult to calculate the timespan covered, but generally, the book begins soon after the death of Joshua and ends in the years just before the entrance of Samuel onto the scene, a period of about three hundred years or so.

These judges were special warrior leaders whom God raised up to rescue and lead His people. Unlike current-day judges who merely oversee legal matters, 2:16 describes the role of the *shophet* or judge: "Then the Lord raised up judges, who saved them out of the hand of those who plundered them." Twelve of these regional military leaders are in this book, and as it progresses, the more flawed they were. Yet the spirit of the Lord came upon these judges, and they delivered the people, which is a reminder that God choses the weak and foolish things in the world to confound the wise.

During the time of the judges, there was great apostasy in Israel. One of the key verses is 2:10b: "And there arose another generation after them who did not know the LORD or the work that he had done for Israel." So tragically we move from the conquest of Joshua to the compromise of Judges. After the death of Joshua, Israel devolved into tribalism and idolatry, as we see in the introduction in chapters 1–2. In chapters 3–16, other than the occasional judge, there is no unifying force, and Israel spiraled further downward toward spiritual and moral anarchy. In fact in the appendix at the end of Judges, chapters 17–21, a refrain is repeated in 17:6 and 21:25: "In those days there was no king in Israel. Everyone did what was right in his own eyes." That pretty much sums up the book of Judges.

The pattern of behavior in Judges is clear: the people rebelled through idolatry and immorality, God brought judgment through pagan oppressors, which caused God's people to cry out for His help, then God mercifully raised up a deliverer—a judge—and the people seem to have repented and turned back to God and experienced some peace. But soon the people fell back into sin, and the sad cycle started over again. In fact, this downward cycle repeats seven times in the book!

Additionally, the tribes fought among themselves, nearly wiping out the tribes of Manasseh (chap. 12) and Benjamin (chaps. 20–21). The book includes many of the most graphic, violent, and disturbing scenes in all Scripture—some in the name of righteousness, others in the name of evil—earning it an *R* rating. Yet in the midst of all this depravity, we meet several heroes of faith: Othniel, Ehud, Shamgar, Deborah, Jephthah, Gideon, Samson—flawed

individuals who answered God's call to deliver the Israelites in sometimes dramatic ways.

The primary message of Judges is God will not allow sin to go unpunished. He disciplined the Israelites for worshipping other gods, disobeying His laws, engaging in blatant immorality, and descending into anarchy at times. Yet because they were His people, He lovingly listened to their cries for mercy and raised up judges to deliver them. Unfortunately, even the judges did not wield sufficient influence to change the nation's downward trajectory.

Remembering the past teaches us many lessons about how to live today, so the book of Judges serves as a warning. The Israelites forgot God and His miraculous deliverances that brought them into their land and the covenant that united them to Him. But God remembered His covenant, and because of His great love for His people, He disciplined His sinful children so that they might return to Him—and He used the judges to help bring it about.

Ruth

The book of Ruth is one of two in the Bible dedicated to a woman—the other book being Esther. We learn in the first verse of Ruth that events took place sometime during the latter period of the judges (Ruth 1:1), around 1100–1000 BC. In fact, the book of Ruth appears as an appendix to the book of Judges, included in the same scroll. According to the Jewish Talmud, the prophet Samuel wrote Ruth. The text itself says nothing of the author, but whoever wrote the book was a master storyteller because Ruth is one of the most beautiful short stories ever written.

The purpose of the book of Ruth is to demonstrate God's providence in the lives of two widows and a farmer and how they played a part in God's master plan of redemption. Their story is told in four chapters.

Chapter 1 opens with a reminder of the dark days of the judges, with Israel under God's judgment. We meet an Israelite family of four in Bethlehem struggling to survive through a famine who made the difficult decision to move to the land of Moab, Israel's ancient enemy, in search of food. But tragedy struck when the father of the family died, leaving Naomi as a widow. The sons married two Moabite women, Ruth and Orpah, but then tragically the sons also died and three widows were left to fend for themselves in this foreign land.

Consequently, Naomi was devastated and had no reason to stay, so she planned to return to Israel. She tried to convince her daughters-in-law to stay behind. Orpah agreed, but Ruth showed remarkable family loyalty to Naomi, and she replied in 1:16, "For where you go I will go, and where you lodge I will lodge. Your people will be my people and your God my God.'" So the two widows returned to Israel, and the chapter concludes with Naomi changing her name to Marah, which means "bitter" in Hebrew, and she hopelessly lamented her tragic circumstances.

Chapter 2 begins with Naomi and Ruth discussing where they're going to find food. It just so happened to be the beginning of the barley harvest, and when Ruth went out to look for food, she picked grain in the field of a man named Boaz. He actually was one of Naomi's relative, and we're told he was a man of noble character. He just so happened to take notice of Ruth, and after finding out more about her, Boaz showed remarkable generosity to her, as a foreign widow in Israel, which shows his obedience to scriptural commands. When Naomi found out that Boaz was involved, her hope was renewed; perhaps he might step up as the kinsman redeemer and help them. So at the end of chapter 2, Naomi began to hope again that her family had a future.

Chapter 3 begins with Naomi and Ruth making a plan to get Boaz to notice her further. So Ruth stopped wearing the clothes of a grieving widow, a sign that she was available to be married. She boldly went to meet Boaz at his farm by night and asked if he would redeem Naomi's family and marry her as the kinsman redeemer. Boaz was amazed by Ruth's loyalty to Naomi and her family, and he called Ruth a woman of noble character, the same term used to describe the ideal woman of Proverbs 31. And he told her to wait until the next day, then he redeemed both Ruth and Naomi legally before the town elders. So the chapter ends with Ruth returning to Naomi, and they mulled over all these promising events.

In chapter 4, the plan all came together but not without some last-minute drama. Boaz discovered a family relative closer to Naomi than he was. He put that guy first in line to redeem the family, but at the last second, this guy found out he must marry Ruth the Moabite and he backed out. Boaz knew Ruth's true character, and so he married her and acquired Naomi's family property as the kinsman redeemer.

The story concludes with a reversal of all of the tragedies from chapter 1. The death of Naomi's husband and her sons was reversed as Ruth married again then gave birth to a new son, which brought great joy to Naomi. Also just as the opening tragedy was followed by a great act of loyalty on Ruth's part, at the end of the book, that was matched by Boaz's act of great loyalty as the kinsman redeemer, which led to Naomi's family finally being restored.

One thing that stands out is how God was barely mentioned in the book of Ruth. While the characters talked about God a few times, the narrator never once mentioned God. And that's why it's such a brilliant story; just as in the book of Esther, God's hand was evident everywhere we look. God's providence was at work behind every scene of this story, weaving together the circumstances and choices of all these ordinary people. Naomi's tragic losses led her to think God was somehow punishing her, but we find out that the whole story is actually about God's plan to restore and bless her and her family. God was working through the widow Ruth, through her loyalty and her boldness, and through the no-nonsense farmer Boaz, who is full of generosity and loyalty, and God providentially used all of these circumstances and choices of these people to save the widow Naomi and her family.

But that's not all that God was up to in the story of Ruth. The book concludes with a big reveal. The genealogy at the end shows how Boaz and Ruth's son, Obed, was the grandfather of King David from whom the Messiah eventually came, the ultimate Kinsman Redeemer. All of a sudden these seemingly ordinary everyday events with these ordinary people in this story were providentially woven into God's magnificent plan of redemption for the whole world. So the book of Ruth prompts us to consider how God might be providentially at work in the ordinary everyday details of our own lives as well and how He is working all things together for good for those who love Him and are called according to His purpose.

1 Samuel

Samuel is widely recognized as the author of at least part of the two-volume work that bears his name. Other contributors to 1 and 2 Samuel are likely the prophetic historians Nathan and Gad (1 Chron. 29:29). Originally, the books of 1 and 2 Samuel were one book in the Hebrew Bible, but the translators of the Greek Septuagint separated them into two, as we have them today. The events of 1 Samuel span approximately one hundred years, from around 1100 BC to 1000 BC. The events of 2 Samuel cover another forty years, to 960 BC.

First Samuel records the history of Israel as they moved from the sporadic rule of judges to being a unified nation under the continuous rule of kings. Sadly the people rejected God as king and demanded a human king like the surrounding nations (1 Sam. 8:5). So 1 Samuel focuses on the establishment of the monarchy.

There are three main characters in the book: Samuel, Saul, and David.

The beginning of the book is set during the spiritual, moral, and political chaos of the book of Judges, with Eli serving. We're introduced to a humble praying woman named Hannah, who was grieved because she was unable to have children. By God's grace, however, she finally has a son, named Samuel, and she rejoiced in chapter 2. Her prayer introduces two key themes: (1) how God opposes the proud and exalts the humble, and (2) one day God will raise up an anointed king for His people. So Hannah's prophetic prayer sets the tone for the entire story that unfolds in 1 Samuel.

Instead of the evil sons of Eli, the Lord exalted humble and obedient Samuel to be the prophetic spiritual leader of Israel and its final judge. Samuel anointed Saul from the lowly tribe of Benjamin as Israel's first king. King Saul, "head and shoulders above the rest," led Israel to early victories but became arrogant and disobedient and lacked integrity. Consequently, God rejected Saul as king, and God instructed Samuel to anoint humble young David as the next king. He was the least son of Jesse of Bethlehem but a man after God's heart (16:1–13).

While Saul remained king to his death, much of 1 Samuel follows David's exploits as a young musician, shepherd, and warrior. We witness his trust in God to grant him an amazing victory over Goliath (17:1–58), his deep friendship with Saul's son Jonathan (18:1–4), and his growing military skills that God blessed with victory after victory (18:5–30). David humbly trusted God and waited patiently for the throne, though often pursued and driven into hiding by Saul, who had descended into jealously and madness. The book concludes with Saul's and his sons' tragic deaths at the hands of the Philistines (31:1–13), which serves as a natural division between 1 Samuel and 2 Samuel.

The two themes from Hannah's prayer at the beginning feature prominently in the overall message of 1 Samuel:

Reversal: Hannah spoke about the fact God exalts the humble but brings low the proud. In the providence of God, humble Hannah's barrenness gave way to children (1:1–28; 2:21); humble Samuel became prophet instead of Eli's worthless sons (2:12; 3:13); Saul rose to prominence though he was from the humble tribe of Benjamin, but when he became arrogant and disobedient, God brought him low. And humble David was anointed king though he was the youngest son of Jesse (16:1–13) because man looks on the outward appearance but God looks on the heart. So despite human evil, God is working out His purposes to oppose the proud and exalt the humble. This book features a series of reversals by God so that His plan could be furthered, showing His sovereignty over all. Speaking of sovereignty, that leads to the second theme Hannah's prophetic prayer introduced: establishing a king:

Kingship: God sovereignly designated a human ruler, David, to shepherd His people as king. The history in 1 and 2 Samuel and

additional prophecy validates the house of David as the legitimate rulers of Israel. It also fulfills Jacob's prophetic promise that the scepter will never depart from Judah, which is the tribe of David (Gen. 49:10). As we all know, Jesus the Messiah came from that Davidic lineage. The royal, risen, returning Son of God will assume His kingship over His people in the age to come in the ultimate fulfillment of God's plan.

Indeed God will sovereignly accomplish His purposes with or without our cooperation. But as was true in the lives of Hannah, Samuel, Saul, and David, our response to God affects our outcome. Will we trust and obey Him as Hannah, Samuel, and David did and live lives marked by His blessing? Or will we, like Saul, try to do it our own way and experience failure? "To obey is better than sacrifice," Samuel told Saul (1 Sam. 15:22). That truth still applies to us today.

2 Samuel

As mentioned in the introduction to 1 Samuel, the translators of the Greek Septuagint divided one book in the Hebrew Bible into two. Second Samuel does not identify its author, but we know it could not be Samuel because he died in the first book that bears his name. Possible writers include the prophets Nathan and Gad, who are prominent in this book, or another of Samuel's protégés from the school of the prophets (1 Sam. 19:18–24). The time period covered is from 1000 to 960 BC.

While 1 Samuel introduces the monarchy of Israel inaugurated with the reign of Saul, the purpose of 2 Samuel is to chronicle the reign of David and the establishment of his dynasty and how that figures in God's unfolding redemptive plan. The book opens as David learned of and lamented the deaths of Saul and Jonathan (2 Sam. 1:19–27). In the beginning, the Lord set David only over the tribe of Judah (2:4) in Hebron, and then after civil war with the house of Saul, David was ultimately anointed king over all of Israel (5:3), uniting all twelve tribes into a nation with the political and religious capital established in Jerusalem.

The book has basically three major sections: (1) David's triumphs, (2) his troubles, and (3) an extended epilogue that ties both books together.

The first ten chapters show David's triumphs. He was victorious in battle, praised by the people, compassionate to the weak, and righteous in God's sight. David danced before the Lord in worship through the streets of Jerusalem as his men brought the ark of the covenant to its new home (6:12–16). David also showed grace to the remaining member of the house of Saul, Mephibosheth, the crippled son of Jonathan (9:7). Yet the biblical writers did not omit flaws of one of the Bible's greatest heroes.

In chapters 11–20, we read of David's troubles. It begins with David's adultery with Bathsheba (11:1–27), his assassination of her husband Uriah, and his attempted cover-up, which was followed by a series of tragedies:

- the child from the illicit union died (12:18),
- David's son Amnon raped his sister Tamar (13:1–39),
- David's son Absalom had Amnon killed (13:28–30),
- Absalom rebelled and overthrew David (15:1–37), and
- Absalom died (18:1–33).

So this section ends as the book began when David lamented over a man who tried to take his life followed by more rebellion and internal strife (chap. 20).

Despite the turmoil in his later years, David continued to experience the Lord's forgiveness

and favor. His genuine sorrow and repentance over his sins revealed the humility of his heart, which sets him in contrast with Saul's arrogance. But the Bible is clear about the fact our choices have consequences that endure.

The last part of the book (chaps. 21–24) is a nonchronological epilogue that contains additional details of David's reign, further pointing out David's vulnerability and recalling in David's song (2 Samuel 22) themes from Hannah's song (1 Samuel 2) which tie the whole two-volume set together in generating hope for a future king to come from David's line.

Speaking of a future king, the key to the book and perhaps the entire biblical story of redemption is in 2 Samuel 7. David proposed to build God a house, a temple in Jerusalem. God declined his proposal and instead promised to build David a house, a dynasty. And in verse 16 God promised David, "And your house and your kingdom shall be made sure forever before me. Your throne shall be established forever."

That divine promise marked the beginning of an additional covenant, the Davidic covenant, in which God promised an everlasting throne to the house of David. That covenant ties into the Abrahamic covenant because we learn that God's plan to bless the nations came through David's line of descendants. A future king was promised who would build God's kingdom here on earth, an eternal kingdom. Obviously, this prophetic promise was ultimately fulfilled in David's greater son, Jesus.

1 Chronicles

We don't know the identity of "the chronicler," as Bible scholars have long referred to the author of this book. Jewish tradition speculates that Ezra the priest could have written 1 and 2 Chronicles, which—like Samuel and

Kings—originally formed one work in the Hebrew Bible. Nothing within the text provides a definitive clue.

But here's the larger question: Because we already have 2 Samuel as well as 1 and 2 Kings, why are the books of Chronicles necessary? The answer is the same reason we have four Gospels: each one gives us a different perspective on the life and ministry Jesus. The books of 1 and 2 Chronicles give us a unique perspective on the kings of Israel and especially the kings of Judah.

Also interesting is the fact that 1 and 2 Chronicles appear last in the Hebrew Bible; they serve as a summary to the entire Old Testament, beginning with Adam and concluding with the return from exile.

The first book of Chronicles has two main parts: genealogies (chaps. 1–9) and a record of David's rule (chaps. 10–29).

First Chronicles begins with nine chapters of genealogies, which may seem boring, but all these lists of names should remind us that God knows each of His children personally. Where we come from, who we are, and what we do are written forever in God's memory. The genealogies are important to the chronicler because he was naming all the key characters in the Old Testament, primarily following two bloodlines: (1) the royal line of Judah that led us to David from whom the Messiah came and (2) the priestly line of Aaron and the priesthood.

The time frame covered in 1 Chronicles 10–29 parallels parts of 2 Samuel and 1 Kings. The chronicler focused on David's reign, including and omitting different events so that he shaped the story for his purposes. For instance, 1 Chronicles leaves out the negative stories about David, like his adultery with Bathsheba, and adds other stories that bolster his image as Israel's greatest king to whom all who follow him are compared in 2 Chronicles.

The chronicler also told the history of Israel from a priestly perspective. There is significant attention to proper worship of Yahweh and adherence to the regulations of His Law. The chronicler even included David's decisions on the proper way to move the ark of the covenant (1 Chronicles 13, 15–16) and detailed descriptions of its placement in Jerusalem. Also included is the story of how David purchased the threshing floor of Ornan the Jebusite, which he then designated as the future site of the temple (21:15–30). Though David truly desired to build the temple, God revealed to him that Solomon would have that honor (17:1–14). Yet as God revealed to Moses the plans for the tabernacle, God revealed to David the plans for the temple, which is another unique story in Chronicles.

Consequently the books of Chronicles, written after the time of the exile, present the stories of David, Solomon, and the kings; so the focus is on those elements of history God wanted the returning Jews to meditate upon, namely: obedience that results in God's blessing, the priority of the temple and priesthood, and the unconditional promises to the house of David that the Messiah fulfilled.

For example, part of the Davidic covenant, which God reiterated in chapter 17, refers to the Messiah who is a descendant of David. Verses 13–14 describe the Son who is established in God's house and whose throne is established forever. This can only refer to Jesus Christ, the greater Son of David. So in 1 and 2 Chronicles, the writer was anticipating a future king and a future temple, which was ultimately fulfilled in and by the Messiah.

Psalms

In Hebrew the book was originally titled *Tehillim*, which literally means "praises" or "praise songs." The English title of "Psalms" originated from the Septuagint's Greek title *Psalmoi*, which means "instrumental songs of praise." This collected hymnbook of the Hebrew people was written by multiple authors and set to music.

Many psalms identify their authors in the title or first line. For example, Moses is named as the author of the oldest psalm (Psalm 90). David's name is associated with seventy-three psalms, nearly half the total, but he could have written more that are simply not directly attributed to him. Interestingly, some of David's psalms have historical notations connecting them with documented events in his life. Not surprisingly, the psalms are most identified with David because he composed so many. Next comes Asaph, who wrote twelve psalms (50, 73–83). Then the descendants of Korah were responsible for eleven (42, 44–49, 84–85, 87–88). Solomon wrote two psalms (72, 127), and Heman and Ethan the Ezrahite were responsible for two others (88 and 89, respectively). The remaining forty-nine psalms do not identify their authors.

As we view the broad chronology of the book of Psalms, the first one dates back to around 1400 BC with Moses, then forward four hundred years to David and then Solomon and all the way to the Ezrahites after the exile. So the psalms were collected, edited, and completed as a unified book after the Jews began their return to the promised land in 537 BC, probably during the time of Ezra, a span of around one thousand years. The book of Psalms features the shortest chapter in the Bible, Psalm 117 (2 verses), and the longest chapter in the Bible, Psalm 119 (176 verses).

The first two psalms set forth two themes echoed through the entire book. Psalm 1 speaks of the blessing that rests on the person who diligently reads, meditates on, and obeys the Torah. Psalm 2 speaks of the blessing on those who take refuge in the promised Messianic King, who will one day reign over all the earth. So the book of Psalms encourages its readers to be faithful to the commands of the Torah even as they await the future Messianic King and His kingdom. Psalms 3–145 are organized into five "books" or collections, and each book concludes with a similar doxology, such as, "Blessed be the LORD, the God of Israel, from everlasting to everlasting! Amen and Amen" (41:13).

The first book of psalms (1–41) speaks of our relationship with Creator God, which corresponds to Genesis. The second book of psalms (42–72) speaks of our redemption by God, which corresponds to the book of Exodus. Book 3 (73–89) speaks of the refuge in God, which corresponds to the book of Leviticus. The fourth book (90–106) speaks of rebellion against God, which corresponds to the book of Numbers. And the fifth book (107–45) speaks of renewal with God through the word and worship and corresponds to Deuteronomy.

These five books are followed by a crescendo of praise with five songs (146–50). Each begin and end with the word "Hallelujah," which is a Hebrew command to "praise Yahweh," culminating with a grand finale of praise in Psalm 150.

Interestingly, Jesus quoted from the book of Psalms more than any other book—eleven times—and at least seventeen psalms are messianic. Psalm 2:1–12 portray the Messiah's triumph and kingdom. Psalm 16:8–11 foreshadow His death and resurrection. Psalm 22 shows us the suffering Savior on the cross and presents detailed prophecies of the crucifixion, all of which were fulfilled perfectly. The glories of the Messiah and His bride are on exhibit in Psalm 45:6–7, while Psalms 72:6–17; 89:3–37; 110:1–7; and 132:12–18 present the glory and universality of His reign. That means when God's covenant people were singing through and meditating on the psalms, they were singing and meditating about Jesus, even if they didn't realize it.

The book of Psalms was not only Jesus's favorite to quote from; it is also the favorite of many believers. One of the biggest reasons is it is so relatable. We find the psalmist going through some of the same experiences we go through. The psalmist's sorrow is our sorrow, his challenges our challenges, his joy our joy. We see ourselves, all our problems and our praise, our trials and our triumphs, in the psalms.

1 Kings

Like the books of 1 and 2 Samuel and 1 and 2 Chronicles, 1 and 2 Kings, which continue the story of Israel's monarchy, originally were one book in the Hebrew Bible. The Greek Septuagint separated them into two parts, and our English versions followed. The author of the book of Kings is unknown, though some commentators have suggested Ezra or Ezekiel, and tradition names Jeremiah as the possible author. One of the prophets is likely given the focus of the book. The entire work covers more than four hundred years, and several source materials were used to compile the narrative, likely while God's people were in Babylonian exile (see 2 Kings).

First Kings opens describing the final days of King David (around 971 BC) and the conspiracies surrounding his successor. Before he died, David charged his son Solomon, who succeeded him:

"I am about to go the way of all the earth. Be strong, and show yourself a man, and keep the charge of the Lord your God, walking in his ways and keeping his statutes, his commandments, his rules, and his testimonies, as it is written in the Law of Moses, that you may prosper in all that you do and wherever you turn, that the Lord may establish his word that he spoke concerning me, saying, 'If your sons pay close attention to their way, to walk before me in faithfulness with all their heart and with all their soul, you shall not lack a man on the throne of Israel.'" (1 Kings 2:2–4)

Those verses are the key to evaluating all the kings who follow in the book of Kings. The charge to the people is similar to those of Moses and Joshua and Samuel: it's a call to remain faithful to the commands of the covenant and to give allegiance to the God of Israel.

As promised, Solomon ascended the throne, and he asked for and God gave him wisdom. In the early years of his reign, Solomon was established as a strong and wise leader. The united kingdom of Israel experienced its "glory days." Its influence, economy, and military power enjoyed its zenith. But the height of Solomon's achievement was the building of God's temple, which is described in great detail. All its gold, silver, and precious stones along with all the ornate designs and symbols echo the garden of Eden—the place where heaven and earth met, the place where God's presence dwells with His people. And God responded dramatically by making His glorious presence known in the new temple. He then appeared to Solomon and reiterated the charge to stay true to the covenant and keep His commandments; otherwise, God would abandon them and bring disaster.

However, Solomon proceeded to make a series of unwise decisions and broke all the rules God had set forth for kings in Deuteronomy 17, and he turned away from the Lord to idols and the seeds of destruction were sown. Shortly after Solomon's death in 931 BC (1 Kings 11:43), the nation was divided into northern (Israel) and southern (Judah) kingdoms. In the north, Samaria ultimately became the capital and rival worship center with its golden calves. In the south, Jerusalem remained the capital and worship center with the temple to YHWH, being ruled by the David's descendants. First Kings follows the history of this divided kingdom through the year 853 BC.

A series of kings who were evil and idolatrous ruled Israel. The nation fell further away from God. Enter the prophet Elijah and his epic confrontations with the wicked King Ahab and Canaanite Queen Jezebel, who persecuted the true prophets and promoted idolatry. Elijah was the forerunner of Christ and the apostles of the New Testament in that God performed seven miraculous acts through Elijah, which proved that his message was true. These miracles demonstrated God's preeminence over His creation, His provision of food, and His power over death itself. When God enabled Elijah to raise the dead son of the widow of Zarephath, she exclaimed, "Now I know that you are a man of God, and that the word of the LORD in your mouth is truth" (17:24). In the same way, God confirmed His word through Christ and the apostles through miracles and signs in the New Testament.

The kings who feared God and remained mostly faithful to the Law—like Asa and Jehoshaphat in Judah—experienced God's blessings. But those kings who departed from the Lord and deviated from the Law experienced His curses, which unfortunately describes all of the kings of the northern kingdom of Israel.

The first book ends with yet another bold prophet, Micaiah, speaking God's truth to wicked King Ahab of Israel and compromised King Jehoshaphat of Judah, but the prophet's words go unheeded, which sums up the sad history of the northern kingdom of Israel and, later, even Judah.

Proverbs

Proverbs is a collection of pithy sayings and brief instructions that encourage wise, God-honoring living. Like the Psalms, Proverbs has multiple authors, but as Psalms is largely identified with David, Proverbs is mostly linked to his son Solomon, who identified himself as the primary author of the book.

At the beginning of his reign, Solomon asked the Lord for wisdom, and God graciously gave it to him—along with everything else. In fact, 1 Kings 4:32 tells us Solomon spoke three thousand proverbs, but the book contains a little less than one thousand. Consequently, most of its contents come from Solomon's collection and were compiled prior to his death in 931 BC. However, King Hezekiah's officials compiled more of Solomon's proverbs (see Proverbs 25–29), which indicates that the book was likely in its final form sometime before the end of Hezekiah's reign in 686 BC.

The theme of Proverbs is found in 1:7: "The fear of the LORD is the beginning of knowledge; fools despise wisdom and instruction." The fear of the Lord refers to our honoring Him with the respect He deserves as God. It means depending on Him with humble trust, living our lives in light of His word, holding Him in the highest regard. Only then, Proverbs teaches, will we discover knowledge and wisdom (see also 9:10).

The root of the Hebrew word for wisdom speaks of skill. It's used in reference to the skilled artisans and craftsman who created the tabernacle and everything in it. Wisdom is the acquired skill of viewing life from God's perspective and then living accordingly.

In the book of Proverbs, Solomon revealed the mind of God on matters great and small. Few topics escaped King Solomon's comment in Proverbs. Matters pertaining to personal conduct and character, sexual relations and marriage, work and leisure, wealth and poverty, discipline and excess, government and godliness are among the many subjects covered in this rich collection of speeches and wise sayings.

Each individual proverb is essentially a couplet, two sayings laid side by side, which employs a literary device called parallelism. The first line states the basic principle, but the second line can either (1) restate it in a different way, (2) contrast it to illustrate it by way of an opposite, or (3) further it to build on it.

The book can be divided into three main parts, each mentioning Solomon's name at its beginning (1:1; 10:1; and 25:1), chapters 1–9, 10–24, and 25–29, which were compiled during Hezekiah's reign, with an addendum or conclusion in chapters 30–31.

There's no real plot or storyline to Proverbs, but think of it as the greatest "how to" manual ever written, offering sound and sensible answers to all manner of life's questions. So there is an undeniable practicality found in this book. You might call Proverbs "practical truth for principled living."

However, wisdom is ultimately found in Christ, the One who is greater than Solomon (Matt. 12:42), "in whom are hidden all the treasures of wisdom and knowledge" (Col. 2:3). In Christ, we find the answer to our search for wisdom. He alone is the source of "wisdom from God, righteousness and sanctification and redemption" (1 Cor. 1:30).

Song of Solomon

The Song of Solomon is well known but a misunderstood part of the Wisdom literature in the Bible. As for the author, these eight chapters of love poetry are attributed to Solomon according to the first verse. In fact, Solomon's name appears several times through the book (1:5; 3:7, 9, 11; 8:11–12). During the past one hundred years or so, however, critics have disputed his authorship, specifically given the fact that he had seven hundred wives and three hundred concubines. Yet in this book, these two lovers seem to be the only ones in the world for each other. While all of that is true, it is not impossible to believe this book of poems is about Solomon's first wife, and perhaps his only true love.

The woman who is the object of his affection is referred to only as the Shulammite, and she has been variously identified, but may have been Abishag, a young Shunammite who served King David in his old age (1 Kings 1:1–4, 15; 2:17–22). It is plausible that Abishag is the Shulammite; we know she was from Shunem, which could be the same place. Also, as David's personal servant, Abishag would have been known to David's son, Solomon. Solomon's half-brother Adonijah attempted to have Abishag as his own wife, and Solomon prevented the union (1 Kings 2:13–25). So the beautiful Abishag could well be the object of Solomon's love poems we call the Song of Solomon.

This song is one of 1,005 that Solomon wrote according to 1 Kings 4:32. The title Song of Songs means this is the best one. As for the date of writing, Solomon most likely wrote this song during the early part of his reign, which places the date of composition around 965 BC.

As for the purpose of writing, again the Song of Solomon is collection of love poems designed to celebrate the beauty of romantic love between a couple as they progress in their courtship, then their marriage and honeymoon, and finally life together as husband and his wife with its inevitable struggles but with love conquering all.

Verses 6–7 of chapter 8 sum it up well:

Set me as a seal upon your heart,
  as a seal upon your arm,
for love is strong as death,
  jealousy is fierce as the grave.
Its flashes are flashes of fire,
  the very flame of the LORD.
Many waters cannot quench love,
  neither can floods drown it.
If a man offered for love,
  all the wealth of his house,
  he would be utterly despised."

The collection of love poems clearly presents marriage as God's good design. A man and woman are to live together within the context of marriage loving each other in spiritual, emotional, and physical intimacy. With all the imagery throughout these poems that speak of the garden, it may be intended to point us back to the original marriage in Genesis between Adam and Eve in the garden of Eden. Certainly, the love relationship and marriage profiled in Song of Solomon models unselfish love, mutual commitment, and uninhibited delight.

The poetry takes the form of a dialogue between lovers, and we can divide the book into three sections: (1) the courtship (1:1–3:5),

(2) the wedding and honeymoon (3:6–5:1), and (3) the maturing marriage (5:2–8:14).

Through history the big question raised by the Song of Solomon is what on earth is love poetry like this doing in the Bible. Some struggle with the explicit nature of the book with its R-rated content. In fact, all this sexual innuendo and intimacy makes many readers uncomfortable, so much so that the Jewish Rabbi Akiva had to vigorously defend the book's place in the Jewish canon even as late as AD 90 at the Council of Jamnia because some did not consider it worthy to be included in Scripture.

Consequently, many Bible interpreters just take Song of Solomon as symbolic of deeper truth. In Jewish tradition it has been read as an allegory with each character symbolic of something or someone higher and holier. So the woman is Israel and the man is Yahweh God, and their love is a symbol of the covenant between God and Israel made at Mount Sinai. Certainly, we will see this type of allegory in the prophets. This allegorical interpretation flowed into Christian tradition, but the characters were swapped. Now Christ is seen as the king, while the church is represented by the Shulammite.

2 Chronicles

We don't know the identity of "the chronicler," as Bible scholars have long referred to the author of this book. Jewish tradition speculates that Ezra the priest could have written 1 and 2 Chronicles, which—like Samuel and Kings—originally formed one work in the Hebrew Bible. Nothing within the text provides a definitive clue.

Again, here's the larger question about Chronicles: Because we already have 2 Samuel as well as 1 and 2 Kings, why are the books of

Chronicles necessary? The answer is the same reason we have four Gospels: each one gives us a different perspective on the life and ministry Jesus. The books of 1 and 2 Chronicles give us a unique perspective on David and his sons who followed him—from Solomon who ruled over all Israel to those who ruled over the southern kingdom of Judah until it fell. Also interesting is the fact that 1 and 2 Chronicles appear last in the Hebrew Bible and serve as a summary of the entire Old Testament, beginning with Adam and concluding with the return from exile. Consequently, the books of Chronicles were likely written between 450 and 425 BC.

Book 2 in our Bibles covers the time from Solomon's ascension to the throne (971 BC) until Judah was invaded and its people carried away into exile in Babylon in 586 BC to the decree of Cyrus allowing their return. The focus of the book is on Judah. The author was more concerned with telling the story of David's reigning descendants than relating the history of the northern kingdom of Israel because of their false worship. The centrality of Jerusalem, where the new temple was built, falls in line with the two-volume book's overarching focus on the priesthood and the worship of God.

While Israel's idolatry and demise, as recorded in the books of Kings, is disappointing, so is the decline of Judah in this book. However, the chronicler chose to emphasize the spiritual reformers in Judah who zealously sought to turn the people back to God. There's new material about how their obedience led to success and God's blessing. To be fair, the chronicler also added new stories about kings who were unfaithful to God, who disobeyed the Torah, broke the covenant, and led their people to worship idols. These kings faced horrible consequences all leading up to their exile, which was a mess of their own making.

So, after the building and dedication of the temple, 2 Chronicles becomes a series of character studies where the author wanted later generations of Israelites to learn from their family history with the hopes they will become faithful to their God. So given that purpose, the goodness of Judah's rulers is stressed. Even Manasseh, one of the most wicked evil kings, repented in the chronicler's unique retelling of history.

Again, 2 Chronicles was probably written in the fifth century BC, following the return of a small band of Jews during the reign of Cyrus after the fall of the Babylonian Empire. Intent on rebuilding the temple and resettling the Holy Land, the little community struggled for years in their fight to reclaim the land and renew their worship at a much smaller temple. Against this discouraging backdrop, the chronicler portrayed their storied past, focusing on the blessings God bestowed when leaders were faithful to obey His word in hopes of encouraging a new generation to do the same.

As with all references to kings and temples in the Old Testament, we see in them a reflection of the true King of kings—Jesus Christ—and of the temple of the Holy Spirit—His people. Even the best of the kings of Israel had the faults of all sinful men and led the people imperfectly. But when the King of kings comes to live and reign on the earth in the millennium, He will establish Himself on the throne of all the earth as the rightful heir of David. Only then will we have a perfect King who will reign in righteousness and holiness, something the best of Israel's and Judah's kings only dreamed about.

The conclusion of the book is unique. It ends with Cyrus, the king of Persia, allowing the Jews to return to the promised land from exile and rebuild the city of Jerusalem and their temple. He says in last line of the book,

"Whoever is among you of all his people, may the LORD his God be with him. Let him go up." That's how the book ends, with an incomplete sentence. Obviously, the author knew about the first return from exile and the stories of Ezra and Nehemiah, but apparently he didn't believe the prophetic hopes of Israel were fulfilled in those events. Consequently, this incomplete ending shows that the author's hope was set on yet another return from exile when the Messiah, the greater Son of David, will finally come to rebuild the temple and restore God's people and His kingdom.

So the book of Chronicles, the final book of the Jewish scriptures, ends by pointing forward. It calls God's people to look back to the past in order to look ahead to the future to find their hope. Chronicles concludes the Old Testament as a story in search of an ending—an ending that will only be fulfilled in the coming of Messiah, King Jesus.

Ecclesiastes

The book of Ecclesiastes is a part of the Wisdom literature of the Bible. The title comes from the Greek Septuagint, and it speaks of a person who calls an assembly together. So it is fitting that the author identified himself by the Hebrew word *qoheleth*, which translates as "preacher." The preacher called himself "the son of David, king in Jerusalem," one who has increased in "wisdom, surpassing all who were over Jerusalem before me" and one who has collected many proverbs (Eccles. 1:1, 16; 12:9). Consequently, all indicators are that King Solomon is the author of Ecclesiastes, and it would have been written before his death in 931 BC.

Solomon set forth his cynical thesis at the beginning: "[V]anity of vanities! All is vanity" (1:2b). The Hebrew word used thirty-eight

times literally means vapor or smoke. Try to grasp it, and you end up empty-handed. Like chasing the wind. That sums up his ultimate disappointment with life from seeking fulfillment in worldly pursuits. Nothing made sense to him because he had tried everything to alleviate his sense of feeling lost in the world. That's why Ecclesiastes offers us a perfect opportunity to understand the emptiness and despair people grapple with who do not know or follow God.

Ecclesiastes 1–7 primarily describe all of the worldly pursuits the preacher tried to find fulfillment in "under the sun" that were ultimately disappointing. He tried scientific discovery (1:10–11), wisdom and philosophy (1:13–18), pleasure and laughter (2:1), alcohol (2:3), architecture (2:4), property (2:7–8), and luxury (2:8). The preacher turned his mind toward different philosophies to find meaning, such as materialism (2:19–20) and even moral codes (including chaps. 8–9). He found that everything was meaningless and wearisome, a temporary diversion that, without God, has no purpose or lasting value, and then you die.

However, even in the writer's long and disappointing pursuit of meaning and significance in life, God remained present. For example, we read that God provides food, drink, and work (2:24); both the sinner and the righteous person live in God's sight (2:26); God's deeds are eternal (3:14); and God empowers people to enjoy His provision (5:19).

Chapters 8–12 of Ecclesiastes describe the preacher's suggestions on how a life should be lived. He came to the conclusion that without God there was no truth or meaning to life. He saw many evils and realized even the best of human achievements were worthless in the long run. Consequently in the final chapter, the preacher admonished his readers to focus on an eternal God instead of temporary pleasure. In

12:1 he urged, "Remember also your Creator in the days of your youth, before the evil days come and the years draw near of which you will say, 'I have no pleasure in them.'" And the closing argument is found in verse 13: "The end of the matter; all has been heard. Fear God and keep his commandments, for this is the whole duty of man."

Ecclesiastes describes a man who worked through this painful process of seeking meaning in life. The world "under the sun," apart from God, is frustrating, cruel, unfair, brief, and "utterly meaningless." While he was initially disappointed, he came out on the other side of this pursuit with a wiser, more seasoned perspective. When we're tempted to give into cynicism about life, we find in the conclusion of Ecclesiastes a man who wisely comes to view the meaning of life through a divinely tinted lens.

God set the desire for eternity in our hearts (3:11), and we know that desire can only be fulfilled in a saving relationship with Jesus Christ, who is the way, the truth and the life (see John 14:6). Jesus came that we might have life and have it in abundance see (John 10:10). Life "under the sun" is meaningless. Only life "in the Son" has ultimate meaning and fulfillment.

Obviously, Solomon didn't have the benefit of the revelation we have on this side of the cross. But he rightly concluded that life is destined to remain meaningless and disappointing apart from God. That's why, in the end, he urged us to fear and obey God so that life will have ultimate meaning.

2 Kings

Again, 1 and 2 Kings were one book in the Hebrew Bible. Because of length, the Greek Septuagint divided it into two parts, and our English Bibles followed. Remember, the author is likely a prophet, and tradition attributes it to Jeremiah, but we do not have definitive evidence as to who specifically wrote it. The book of 2 Kings continues the history of the divided kingdom, picking up the story around 853 BC, both summarizing and evaluating the rulers in the northern and southern kingdoms as well as relating stories about the prophets God sent to engage them.

After telling stories from the ministries of the prophets Elijah and Elisha, the writer tells us how the northern kingdom was shaken up by a bloody revolution King Jehu started (he also destroyed Ahab's family). Although God first commissioned Jehu, his violence inspired a downward spiral of political assassinations and rebellions from which Israel never recovered. And it all led up to 2 Kings 17, when the empire of Assyria swooped down and took out the northern kingdom altogether; the capital city of Samaria was conquered, and the Israelites were exiled and scattered throughout the ancient world. Chapter 17 is key because the story is paused, and the writer offered a prophetic reflection blaming the downfall of the northern kingdom on the idolatry and covenant unfaithfulness of Israel and its kings. So God allowed them to face the consequences of their decisions. The final movement of the book tells the story of the lone southern kingdom.

For a few more chapters of the book, about 135 years, only Judah remained intact. But then Assyria suffered a stunning fall to the Babylonians, who took the Assyrian capital of Nineveh in 612 BC. By 605 BC, Babylon dominated Judah, took some captives away, and in 586 BC Babylon destroyed Jerusalem and took additional prisoners into captivity. Many people who were considered valuable to the invaders, such as the prophet Daniel and members of the royal family, were taken to Babylon early on. By the end of Kings, the majority of God's people were in captivity, no longer dwelling in the promised land. Those remaining were scattered and decimated by their enemies, some opting to return to Egypt, including Jeremiah who did so under protest. The book ends with an epilogue of sorts, giving a hopeful word about Jehoiachin—a descendant of David and Judah's last true king before Babylon officials installed a series of puppet rulers.

The time period this book covers includes the emergence of the first writing prophets in Israel. God sent Amos and Hosea to the people of Israel, while Joel, Isaiah, Micah, Nahum, Habakkuk, Zephaniah, and Jeremiah prophesied in Judah, both groups calling the people to repentance and warning them of God's coming judgments. The author devoted extensive space to Elisha's ministry after Elijah was taken to heaven, giving special attention to the numerous miracles Elisha performed. While Elijah performed seven miracles at the hand of God, Elisha asked for a double portion of His spirit, and indeed fourteen of his miracles were recorded. In fact, many of the miracles of these two prophets foreshadow miracles in the ministry of Jesus, such as raising the dead, healing lepers, and feeding multitudes.

As to the evaluation of the kings, none of the rulers of Israel were described as having done right in God's eyes. Indeed, each led the people deeper into idolatry and immorality. Several of Judah's kings were mostly righteous, notably Joash, Uzziah, Hezekiah, and Josiah, though each had his own failures. Hezekiah led a sweeping revival and reforms and, notably, trusted God to hold off the Assyrians. Josiah later instituted a spiritual reformation based on the rediscovery of God's Law. Yet neither effort was enough to resist the inexorable judgment of

God coming upon both nations, whose leaders and people were predominantly bent on idolatry and immorality.

Despite repeated warnings from God's prophets to turn from their wicked ways and return to God, the people continued to live in rebellion. To their regret, they did not believe that God would allow foreign invaders to ravage and ruin their nation. Yet God did not forget His promise to David, either. God saved a remnant from among the people and kept the royal line intact so that one day His people could return to their land to await the promised Messiah and greater Son of David.

Joel

Joel's name means "Yahweh is God," so his name is literally a faith declaration in the age of idolatry that is parallel to our New Testament faith declaration "Jesus is Lord." The book of Joel has been dated anywhere from 850 BC, which would make him one of the first of the Minor Prophets (one hundred years before Jonah, Amos, Hosea), to around 440 BC (the time of Ezra and Nehemiah) or even later. Complicating the dating is the fact no kings are mentioned. Compounding the mystery is that Joel quoted or alluded to the words of so many other prophets (Jonah, Amos, Isaiah, Micah, Jeremiah, Ezekiel, Zephaniah, Obadiah, and Malachi, the last of the Minor Prophets). Joel's reference to the Greeks in 3:6 makes some scholars think the book was written after exile and return to the land.

However, Joel did mention the temple in Jerusalem, which was destroyed in 586 BC and not rebuilt until 516 BC. Consequently, this makes some scholars conjecture that the prophet Joel lived and prophesied well before the destruction of the first temple and exile of

God's people, but that a later editor, who collected his work, added all the allusions to later prophets that seem to reflect a later period. So the book of Joel is like Proverbs, most of which Solomon wrote, but the book was finished by King Hezekiah's wise men some two hundred years later. Bottom line is, we really don't know definitively when the prophet lived or his book was finalized.

Regardless, the recurring theme of the day of the Lord is at the forefront. Joel referred to it six times in this short book. It can be both immediate, reflecting God's remedial judgment on His people, and even punishment of other nations, and the day of the Lord can be ultimate, reflecting the great tribulation and the return of Christ to rule from a restored Jerusalem on a renewed earth. In chapters 1 and most of 2, it is immediate. But at the end of chapter 2 and all of chapter 3, the day of the Lord is more ultimate, looking forward in history to the end times.

Under this general theme of the day of the Lord, Joel talked about three main events:

First, he saw a vision of literal famine and a plague of locusts that descended on the promised land in chapter 1. This invasion destroyed the crops and fruit-bearing vines and trees. In similar terms, a second cataclysmic event followed the first.

Second, in chapter 2 Joel used the locust plague as a symbol of an invading human army, marching to destroy the nation, and he viewed all of this as divine judgment coming because of Judah's sins. Consequently, the required response was to repent. In view of these two cataclysmic events, Joel appealed to all the people and especially the priests of the land to fast and weep and humble themselves as they cried out for God's forgiveness in the temple (1:13–14).

In 2:12–17, Joel called on them to return to the Lord with all their hearts with fasting, weeping, and mourning, to "rend your hearts and not your garments," and to call a solemn assembly and cry out to the Lord. In fact, Joel later promised, "everyone who calls on the name of the LORD shall be saved" (2:32), which Paul picked up in Romans 10:13. Consequently, if they responded with true repentance, there would be renewed material and spiritual blessings for the nation (2:18–27). But the day of the Lord was coming in a more immediate sense in chapter 1 and most of chapter 2.

The third key event, near the end of chapter 2, was the promised outpouring of God's Spirit (2:28–29). Peter referenced the initial fulfillment of this in Acts 2, quoting Joel's prophecy as having taken place at Pentecost. But Joel also saw that event as a harbinger of the last days, leading up to the ultimate day of the Lord. So 2:18–3:21 contains God's answer to the call for humble repentance with prophecies of ultimate judgment and restoration.

First, there was physical restoration (2:21–27). God said, "I will restore to you the years that the swarming locusts has eaten." Second, God said there was spiritual restoration (2:28–32). God promised, "I will pour out my Spirit on all flesh; your sons and your daughters shall prophesy, your old men shall dream dreams, and your young men shall see visions" (v. 28). Third, there was national restoration after the great tribulation and God's judgment on the nations (3:1–21). God said, "But Judah shall be inhabited forever, and Jerusalem to all generations. . . . [F]or the LORD dwells in Zion" (vv. 20–21). What great and precious promises for those who returned to the Lord with all their hearts and bowed themselves in humble repentance before the Lord!

Amos

Amos was a shepherd and a fig tree farmer (7:14–15) in the village of Tekoa in the southern kingdom of Judah, but God called him to be a prophet to the prosperous northern kingdom of Israel. According to 1:1, Amos began his ministry two years before an earthquake that Josephus also referenced as occurring the year Judah's King Uzziah usurped the role of the priests, tried to burn incense in the temple, and was stricken by leprosy. Scholars believe that happened in 750 BC, so that means Amos prophesied around 752 BC, only thirty years before the Assyrians invaded and wiped out Israel.

At that time, Jeroboam II ruled Israel. He was a successful leader who won many battles, expanded their territory, and generated lots of wealth, but he did what was evil in the eyes of God. He continued the worship of the golden calves in Bethel and Dan, and all the prosperity and wealth led to apathy, which in turn led to injustice and mistreatment of the poor. God put a burden in the heart of Amos to speak out about it, so he trekked north to Bethel and declared God's word to the people. Consequently, the book of Amos is a collection of his sermons, poems, and visions compiled to preserve God's message of judgment and call to repent to the northern kingdom, and it's a message we still need to hear today.

The outline of the book of Amos is straightforward. Chapters 1 and 2 contain a series of judgment messages to the surrounding nations and culminates with a more detailed condemnation of Israel. Chapters 3 to 6 are a collection of prophetic poems that declare God's message to repent given to the people of Israel and its leadership. Chapters 7 to 9 contain a series of visions Amos experienced that depict God's

coming judgment on Israel, which he referred to as the "day of the Lord."

Other than his bare-knuckled, no-nonsense preaching, which we can greatly appreciate, Amos included moments of praise to God as the Almighty Creator (4:13; 5:8; 9:5–6). And the book can be divided into three main themes.

The first theme has to do with injustice. Amos exposed the religious hypocrisy of Israel's leaders and the wealthy by describing how they faithfully attended worship, gave their offerings and sacrifices, but neglected the poor and ignored injustice—Amos said it's all a sham. God actually hated their worship because it was totally disconnected from how they treat people. God says a real relationship with Him will transform our relationships with others. Amos declared the solution in 5:24: "But let justice roll down like waters, and righteousness like an ever-flowing stream," a verse Martin Luther King Jr. often quoted and the only Scripture on his monument in Washington, DC.

The psalmist declared that justice and righteousness are the foundation of God's throne, so these two words were important for Amos and all of the prophets. Righteousness is God's standard of what is right, and justice refers to the application of that standard in concrete actions that we take to correct injustice and live out righteousness. God calls for both to flow out of our lives in abundance.

The second theme has to do with idolatry that led to immorality. In the northern kingdom, Amos not only called them out for the worship of the golden calves in the rival temples but also for worshipping other false gods such as Baal and Asherah (2:7–8) and Sikkuth and Kiyyun. (In 5:26, Septuagint has Moloch for Sikkuth and Rephan (an Egyptian deity related to the planet Saturn) for Kiyyun, gods of prosperity, sexual immorality, climate change, and war.) Worship of these gods always led to injustice and immorality because they didn't require the same degree of justice and righteousness as the God of Israel. In fact, their very worship practices required immorality. That's why God called His people to repent and return to Him in 5:4: "For thus says the LORD to the house of Israel: "Seek me and live." Then in verse 14, He said to Israel: "Seek good, and not evil, that you may live; and so the LORD, the God of hosts, will be with you, as you have said." Our belief and behavior are inextricably linked. They professed to believe in God but lived like practical atheists, and God says we can't do that. Repent.

The final theme is the inescapability of the day of the Lord—a day of coming judgment. The popular conception of the event was God would judge other peoples, so the Israelites said bring it on. But Amos's message was that the day of the Lord was going to be a great and terrible act of judgment and justice *on Israel*. Specifically, Amos predicted that a powerful nation would come and conquer and decimate their cities and take the people away into exile, and we know his prediction came true some thirty years later.

Like many predictions in the Bible, there are multiple levels of fulfillment. Immediate fulfillment was judgment in the form of the Assyrian armies invading, conquering and exiling the people of Israel. But there's going to be a future fulfillment of the day of the Lord. In the final paragraph of Amos 9, we get a glimmer of hope. God said out of the ruins of Israel's judgment, He will one day restore the house of David. In other words, He's going to bring the future Messianic King from David's line and rebuild the family of God's people, which will also include people from all nations. So the devastation caused by Israel's sin and God's judgment

will be reversed on that day of the Lord in the future, a day of renewal.

So through the prophecy of Amos, we still hear God's call to repent. We learn from Israel's injustice, idolatry, and immorality, which resulted in an inescapable judgment, to seek God and seek good, which should always lead to justice and righteousness toward our neighbor.

Jonah

The book of Jonah is a historical account of a dramatic episode in the life of the prophet that eventually led to one of the greatest awakenings in the Bible among a pagan people. Jonah is only identified in the book as the son of Amittai. Yet in 2 Kings 14:25, we learn he came from Gath-hepher, which was a town near Nazareth in what became known as Galilee in Israel. We also learn Jonah spoke a positive prophecy regarding Israel's successful military expansion under King Jeroboam II, who ruled forty-one years beginning around 783 BC. However, Jeroboam II is identified as an evil ruler (2 Kings 14:24) whose unjust regime was the prophet Amos's target of condemnation.

Continuing in the tradition of Elijah and Elisha, God called Jonah to deliver His message to a foreign audience, in this case to Nineveh, the capital city of Assyria. In a few decades, Assyria would become a world power and sweep south to destroy the northern kingdom of Israel. Even in Jonah's day, they were viewed as a potential threat, as Joel predicted years before. Yet it was to this hostile pagan nation God sent Jonah with a warning and declared, "their evil has come up before me" (1:2). We know from history that the Assyrians put fishhooks into their victims and dragged them off into captivity; other victims they flayed alive then decorated walls with human skins; others they beheaded then stacked the skulls into pyramids. They were cruel and ruthless people. So it is not surprising that God asked his prophet to go speak a word of judgment to these pagan people. What is surprising is how Jonah responded to God's call.

The book easily divides into four sections that align with the four chapters:

In chapter 1, Jonah disobeyed God's direct command, instead hopping on a ship headed in the opposite direction of Nineveh. His destination was Tarshish, the farthest known western outpost of civilization. In fact, Jonah went "away from the presence of the LORD" (1:3). But Jonah learned you can't run from God. The Lord hurled a storm at the ship, and as the passengers feared for their lives, the pagan sailors showed more respect for God than His prophet. Jonah was apparently determined to die rather than obey God, so he encouraged the sailors to throw him overboard to appease God's anger.

In chapter 2, God didn't let Jonah off the hook so easily, preparing a giant fish to swallow the rebellious prophet. Trapped in the belly of this fish, Jonah cried out to God for deliverance in a prayer reminiscent of many psalms. And the Lord responded by prompting the fish to vomit Jonah onto dry land.

In chapter 3, God gave Jonah a second chance, renewing the call to preach to the pagans in Nineveh. This time Jonah obeyed but only in a minimalist sense. He went into the Assyrian city a day's journey, simply declaring, "Yet forty days, and Nineveh shall be overthrown!" (3:4). When this word from God reached the king of Assyria, Ashurdan III (772–754 BC) repented in sackcloth and ashes; he even issued a decree to the inhabitants of Nineveh to call out mightily to God and to turn from their evil and violent behavior in the hopes God might turn from His anger so that they might not perish (vv. 6–9). Ironically, these pagan Assyrians feared God

more than His prophet did. Their repentance moved God's heart, and He stayed His hand of judgment (v. 10).

In chapter 4, instead of being elated with their repentant response, Jonah was angry at God. Instead of destroying them, God let them off the hook. Disgusted, Jonah essentially told God, "I knew you would be compassionate and merciful to these Assyrian pagans," loosely echoing Exodus 34:6, "and that's why I ran in the opposite direction." Then he prayed in verse 3: "O LORD, please take my life from me, for it is better for me to die than to live." And God called him out for being angry.

But there's one last episode. Jonah set up a bivouac outside Nineveh, apparently still hoping for God's judgment to fall on the city. Then in 4:6, we read God appointed a plant to give Jonah shade, which made Jonah happy. But the next day, God appointed a worm to attack the plant so that it withered. He then appointed a scorching east wind and searing sun to beat down on Jonah's head so that he was faint. Once again, Jonah prayed, "It is better for me to die than to live" (v. 8).

God essentially replied, "Let me get this straight, you care more about a plant than you do about all these people?" How convicting is that? God gives us proper perspective to close out the book: "And should not I pity Nineveh, that great city, in which there are more than 120,000 persons who do not know their right hand from their left, and also much cattle?" (v. 11). So the final question is not only for this disobedient, unloving prophet who had his priorities upside down; it is a word directed to us as well.

One final irony regarding the book of Jonah: Jesus identified Himself with the prophet. Indeed, Jonah is one of only four prophets Jesus quoted, along with Isaiah, Daniel and Zachariah. Specifically, Jesus used Jonah's "three days and three nights in the belly of the great fish" to foreshadow His own death and entombment "in the heart of the earth" before his triumphant resurrection (see Matt. 12:39–41). Consequently, Jonah provides a vital link in the chain of Old Testament prophecies that offer a compelling preview of Messiah's death and resurrection literally hundreds of years before these events happened.

Hosea

The prophet Hosea, whose name means "Yahweh saves," had a compelling ministry in that his whole life circumstances communicated God's message. Many other prophets performed symbolic acts that carried the word of the Lord, but Hosea was uniquely directed by God to marry a bride named Gomer described as "a wife of whoredom" (Hosea 1:2), a woman who bore Hosea three children, two sons and a daughter (1:4, 6, 9). So God used Gomer's unfaithfulness and the very names of Hosea's children to speak about how heartbroken He was over the Israel's unfaithfulness.

Hosea's lengthy ministry during the reigns of several kings of Judah and of Israel (1:1) made him a contemporary of Amos, who also prophesied to the northern kingdom, as well as Isaiah and Micah, who prophesied to the southern kingdom. Hosea prophesied ruin during the latter half of the eighth century BC, specifically during Israel's final years, directing his prophetic warnings to its people and rulers, Jeroboam II, and his son, Zechariah (Hosea 1:4; 2 Kings 15:8–12).

Again, the first three chapters describe Hosea's broken marriage to a woman named Gomer, who committed adultery. She left and got herself in trouble. But God instructed Hosea in 3:1 to go buy her back and bring her home and make her his wife again. Then God said that all of this—the broken and restored marriage, the children—it's all a symbolic message telling the story of God's relationship to Israel. God had been like a faithful husband to Israel, rescued them out of slavery, brought them to Mount Sinai, entered into a covenant with them. He asked them to be faithful to Him alone. But then He brought Israel into the promised land with all its abundance, and instead of faithful worship of God alone, they worshipped Baal and Asherah. So God had a legitimate reason to end the covenant and divorce Israel for adultery. Instead He said that He would pursue Israel again and renew His covenant with them. Why? It's purely because of His own love, compassion, and faithfulness.

Hosea then spelled out what all this means. He said the consequences for Israel's rebellion meant imminent defeat and exile, but there was hope for future restoration. One day Israel would once again repent and come back to worship their God. And Hosea said God would place over them a new Messianic King from the line of David who will bring His blessing. So this opening section introduces all the main ideas of the book. Israel had rebelled, and God was going to bring severe consequences, but God's own covenant love and mercy were more powerful than Israel's sin.

In the two remaining sections of the book (chaps. 4–10 and 11–14), the prophet Hosea's explored these themes in more depth.

In chapters 4–10, Hosea explored the causes and effects of Israel's unfaithfulness. They didn't know God intimately, they broke his Ten Commandments indiscriminately, and by worshipping other gods, their worship of Yahweh was simply hypocrisy. This propensity for idolatry meant the Israelites lived as if they were not God's people. And though God told them as much through the birth of Hosea's third child, Lo-ammi, meaning "Not My People," He also reminded them that He would ultimately restore their relationship with Him, using the intimate and personal language of "sons" to describe His wayward people (1:9–10; 11:1).

That brings us to the final section in chapters 11–14, where Hosea gave us an ancient Israelite history lesson to show how God's people had been unfaithful from the beginning. So what hope did Hosea offer? Well we know from chapter 3 that God was going to do something to save and restore His people, and that's what the concluding chapters explore.

But that brings us back to the beginning with the way God intentionally wove His message into Hosea's family life. By marrying Gomer, a woman he knew would eventually betray his trust and commit adultery, and by giving his children names that sent messages of judgment on Israel, Hosea's prophetic word flowed out of his broken home life. The cycle of repentance, redemption, and restoration evident in Hosea's prophecy and played out in his broken and restored marriage (1:2; 3:1–3) reminds us that the Scriptures are not simply a collection of abstract statements and truth propositions with no relation to real life. No, they work their way into our day-to-day, flesh-and-blood circumstances, speaking truth to issues that impact all our actions and relationships.

The book of Hosea provides an unforgettable example of God's love for His people who have broken His heart by leaving Him for worthless idols, and it also shows us what forgiveness and restoration look like in a covenant relationship. Certainly, God brings judgment on those who turn from Him, but Hosea's powerful act of restoration within his own marriage sets the bar high for us. The book of Hosea illustrates that no one should be beyond the offer

of our forgiveness because no one is outside of God's offer of forgiveness.

But in the end, Hosea offers us a powerful message about God, who with a broken heart continues to love us in spite of our sin, who made the ultimate sacrifice to buy us back, and who longs to restore us to a love relationship with Himself.

Isaiah

Like almost all the prophetic books, the book of Isaiah takes its name from its principle writer, whose name means "Yahweh is salvation." However, much of the scholarship for the past couple of centuries has proposed the book was written by multiple writers, dividing the book into three sections: 1–39, 40–55, and 56–66. And these divisions are based on a scholarly denial of predictive prophecy. This position not only proposes to limit the power of God to communicate with His people about the future but also ignores the wide variety of specific, predictive claims about Jesus Christ scattered throughout the book.

Isaiah, considered by many as the Prince of the Prophets, was a court prophet and married to a prophetess who bore him at least two sons (Isa. 7:3; 8:3), both of whom had names that carried God's message, not unlike Hosea's children. Isaiah prophesied from 739 to 681 BC primarily to the kingdom of Judah under the reign of several kings, beginning with Uzziah, then Jotham, Ahaz, and Hezekiah (1:1). Tradition tells us Isaiah met his death under a fifth king, the wicked Manasseh. As early as the second century, Justin Martyr identified Isaiah as one of the prophets whose death is described in Hebrews 11:37; specifically, the prophet Isaiah was the one who was "sawn in two."

Isaiah witnessed Judah go through times of spiritual rebellion as they did under Ahaz but also times of spiritual revival as they did under Hezekiah. So Isaiah proclaimed first of all a message of God's judgment. He warned corrupt leaders that their rebellion against God, especially those in covenant with God, would come at a cost. Namely that God was going to use the great empires of Assyria and later Babylon to judge Jerusalem if they persisted in idolatry, immorality, and injustice. Consequently, they should repent.

But Isaiah's message of judgment was combined with a message of hope. When Assyria threatened Judah with destruction, they cried out to God, and in mercy, He spared them. Isaiah also proclaimed that God would one day fulfill all of His covenant promises, and specifically, He would send a king from David's line to establish God's kingdom. So Isaiah's message was both one of repentance from sin as well as the hopeful expectation of God's deliverance.

In fact, the book generally divides along those two thematic lines:

Chapters 1–39 develop Isaiah's call to repentance and warning of judgment, and it all culminated at the end of chapter 39 with the prediction of Jerusalem's tragic demise and the exile of God's people to Babylon. But in chapters 1 to 39, there's also a message of hope that after the exile God's covenant promises would all be fulfilled.

In chapters 40–66, Isaiah expounded on that promise of hope. He predicted a return from exile and even named the deliverer God would raise up, Cyrus of Persia, who allowed the exiles to return to their land (45:1). Looking even further into the future, God spoke of a renewed Jerusalem where God's kingdom would be restored through the future Messianic King and all nations would come together in peace.

Perhaps most importantly, the book of Isaiah provides us with the most comprehensive prophetic picture of Jesus Christ in the entire Old Testament. It includes the full scope of His life: From the announcement of His coming by the forerunner (40:3–5), His virgin birth (7:14), His proclamation of the good news (61:1), His healing ministry (35:5–6), His sacrificial suffering and death in order to pay for our sins (52:13–53:12) to His resurrection (53:10–11) as well as His return to claim His own (60:2–3).

Additionally, the Messiah will one day govern the nations in justice and righteousness (9:7; 32:1), bringing peace (11:6–9) as the Prince of Peace (9:6). Through the rule of Messiah, a renewed Israel will be a light to all the nations (42:6; 55:4–5). The Messiah's kingdom on earth (chaps. 65–66) is the goal toward which Isaiah pointed.

The book of Isaiah presents the coming Christ to us in undeniable detail seven hundred years before His birth, life, death, and resurrection. Because of these and numerous other messianic texts in Isaiah, the book stands as a powerful testament of hope in the Lord, the One who saves and delivers His people who put their trust in Him. Isaiah 12:2 proclaims that theme: "Behold, God is my salvation; I will trust, and will not be afraid; for LORD GOD is my strength and my song, and he has become my salvation."

Micah

Micah was a prophet from the rural town of Moresheth, near Philistine territory southwest of Jerusalem. A contemporary of Isaiah and Hosea, Micah stated in his introduction to the book that he prophesied during the reigns of Jotham, Ahaz, and Hezekiah in Judah (757–699 BC). So he basically went on a sixty-year-long roller coaster ride during the reigns of good kings alternating with a really bad one.

However, Micah not only prophesied to Jerusalem and leaders of the southern kingdom but also to Samaria and the northern kingdom during the string of ungodly kings who drove Israel into the ground. In fact, Micah prophesied during the years surrounding the fall of Israel to the Assyrian Empire (722 BC), an event he also predicted (Micah 1:6).

There are three basic sections to his prophecy:

Chapters 1–3 contain messages of judgment, directed at both Israel and Judah because of their idolatry, immorality, and injustice.

Chapters 4–5 are mostly prophecies concerning the coming Messiah and the Messianic kingdom. In fact, George Washington's favorite verse was Micah 4:4: "they shall sit every man under his vine and under his fig tree, and no one shall make them afraid, for the mouth of the LORD of hosts has spoken." For Washington, an American ideal is peace and prosperity under the benevolent providence of God.

Chapters 6–7 depict a courtroom scene in which God's people stand trial before their Creator for turning away from Him (6:1–7:20). God indicted them that in spite of the fact He cared for them, they cared only for themselves, went their own way. But the book of Micah concludes with the prophet's resolve to look to the Lord as the only source of salvation and mercy (7:7), pointing the people toward an everlasting hope in their everlasting God. And we read in the end that they will return to him and God will receive them.

In fact, Micah declared:

Who is a God like you, pardoning iniquity
and passing over transgression
for the remnant of his inheritance?
He does not retain his anger forever,
because he delights in steadfast love.

He will again have compassion on us;
he will tread our iniquities underfoot.
You will cast all our sins
into the depths of the sea. (7:18–19)

In the last verse of the book, he recalled the promise to Abraham as the basis for the continuation of the relationship.

You will show faithfulness to Jacob
and steadfast love to Abraham,
as you have sworn to our fathers
from the days of old." (7:20)

Most notably, the book of Micah provides one of the most significant prophecies about the birth of Jesus Christ's in all the Old Testament, pointing some seven hundred years before Christ's birth to His birthplace of Bethlehem and to His eternal nature (5:2).

But you, O Bethlehem Ephrathah,
who are too little to be among the clans
of Judah,
from you shall come forth for me
one who is to be ruler in Israel,
whose coming forth is from of old,
from ancient days. (5:2)

Surrounding Micah's prophecy of Jesus's birth is one of the most clear and compelling pictures of the future under the reign of the Messiah, the Prince of Peace (5:5). This future kingdom will be characterized by the presence of many nations living with one another in peace and security (4:3–4) and coming to Jerusalem to worship the reigning King, that is, Jesus Himself (4:2).

In the meantime, we would do well to live as God requires in Micah 6:8—"to do justice, and to love kindness, and to walk humbly with your God."

Appendix 2: Biblical Chronology Timeline

Timeline*	Bible Books	Personalities
	Genesis (Events ? BC–1805 BC)	Adam & Eve
		Noah
		Abraham (2166–1991 BC)
	Job (Events 2100–1900 BC)	Isaac (2066–1886 BC)
2000 BC		Jacob (2006–1859 BC)
		Joseph (1915–1805 BC)
1750 BC		
1500 BC		
	Exodus (Events 1805–1445 BC)	Moses (1526–1406 BC)
	Leviticus (1445? BC)	Aaron (1529–1406? BC)
	Numbers (Events 1445–1407 BC)	
	Deuteronomy (Events 1406 BC)	
	Joshua (Events 1406–1380 BC)	Joshua (1490–1380? BC)
	Judges (Events 1380–1060? BC)	Deborah (1360–1300? BC)
1250 BC		Gideon (1250–1175? BC)
		Jephthah (1200–1150? BC)
		Samson (1120–1060? BC)
	Ruth (Events 1150–40? BC)	Ruth (1175–1125? BC)
	1 Samuel (Events 1105–1010? BC)	Samuel (1105–1025? BC)
		Saul (Rule 1050–1010 BC)
	2 Samuel & 1 Chronicles (1010–970)	David (Rule 1010/1003–970 BC)
1000 BC		
	Psalms (1440–537? BC)	
	Proverbs, Song, Ecclesiastes	Solomon (Rule 970–931 BC)
	1 Kings (Events 970–848 BC)	Rehoboam & Jeroboam (931 BC)
		Ahab (874–53) & Elijah (862–52)
	2 Chronicles (Events 970–538)	
	2 Kings (853–561 BC)	Elisha (850?–798? BC)
	Joel (Around 850? BC)	
	Amos (783–746 BC)	Jeroboam II (793?–753 BC)
750 BC	Jonah (775–55? BC)	
	Hosea (750–722 BC)	
	Isaiah (740–681 BC)	Hezekiah (715–686 BC)
	Micah (737–696 BC)	

* Source: Biblical Illustrator Old and New Testament Time Line (Nashville: LifeWay Christian Resources, 2012); available at LifeWay.com/biblicalillustrator.

Appendix 3: How to Pray

Most Americans say they pray, but not as many pray the way Jesus did, the way He taught His disciples to pray. Fewer still really know the power in prayer God gave us to impact our families, communities, nation, and world. Prayer is our lifeline to God, our means of communicating with our heavenly Father. It develops our relationship—our friendship, fellowship, and intimacy with Him. In prayer we experience God and are "filled with the Spirit" (see Eph. 5:18–21). God uses the prayers of faithful men, women, boys, and girls to heal broken lives and strengthen families, churches, communities, and even nations. He uses our prayers to advance His kingdom on earth (Daniel 9; Acts 4:23–31). He wants to use all believers!

The Essence of Prayer

Prayer is simply talking with God—about anything and everything. He is our Maker, Father, Savior, Provider, and Counselor; our Master, Healer, Guide, and Friend. Christ died for our sins and rose from the dead to sit at the right hand of God the Father, where He is praying for us right now (Heb. 10:12). His Spirit now lives within us and helps us to pray (1 John 4:16).

The Priority of Prayer

Jesus spent time alone with God regularly drawing strength from the Father and seeking His will for every decision (Luke 6:12–13;

22:39–44). His disciples asked Jesus to teach them how to pray (Luke 11:1–13). The apostles knew that prayer and obedience were the keys to Christ's life and ministry and were determined to follow His example: "[W]e will devote ourselves to prayer and to the ministry of the word" (Acts 6:4). Too few American men pray today, even pastors and leaders! Yet strong praying men are the norm in Scripture. Our families, churches, and nation need men who will make prayer a priority today (1 Tim. 2:8).

The Practice of Prayer

Scripture teaches, "Pray without ceasing" (1 Thess. 5:17); "Praying at all times" (Eph. 6:18); "Always to pray and not lose heart" (Luke 18:1). Below are some helps to get you started. No one can beat the Lord's Prayer. It is an outline of key themes to guide our prayer lives:

> "Our Father in heaven,
> hallowed be your name.
> Your kingdom come,
> your will be done,
>   on earth as it is in heaven.
> Give us this day our daily bread,
> and forgive us our debts,
>   as we also have forgiven our debtors.
> And lead us not into temptation,
>   but deliver us from evil." (Matt. 6:9–13)

In the book of Psalms and throughout Scripture, God has sprinkled prayers/patterns for us to learn from. Here is a simple, popular acronym to help jog our memories.

P-R-A-Y:

Praise: Our Father in heaven, hallowed be your name.

Repent: And forgive us our debts, as we also have forgiven our debtors.

Ask: Give us this day our daily bread, and forgive us our debts, as we also have forgiven our debtors. And lead us not into temptation, but deliver us from evil.

Yield: Your kingdom come, your will be done, on earth as it is in heaven.

Praying through Scripture

God also talks to us. The Bible is His Word (2 Tim. 2:15; 3:16). Bible in hand, we should pray God's promises back to Him and claim them for our families, our work, our finances, and our nation (1 Tim. 2:1–8; 1 John 5:14–15).

Scriptures to Pray as a Man: Joshua 1:8; 1 Timothy 3:1–15; 1 Chronicles 12:32; 1 Timothy 6:1–12; 1 Corinthians 16:13; Romans 12:1–21; Micah 6:8; John 4:24; Acts 2:38: 1 Kings 2:2; Ephesians 5:25–28; Genesis 2:24; 1 Peter 3:7; Ephesians 4:26–27; Matthew 5:32; Proverbs 5:19; 1 Corinthians 6:18; Deuteronomy 4:8–10; 11:18–21; Exodus 34:5–8; Psalm 127:3–5; Matthew 7:11; Ephesians 6:4; Proverbs 22:6; Luke 11:11–12; Hebrews 12:5–7.

Scriptures to Pray as a Woman: Matthew 22:36–40; Proverbs 31:30; 1 Peter 3:1–3; Ephesians 5:26; Ephesians 4:15, 29; 1 Timothy 3:11; Ephesians 5:22, 24; 1 Peter 3:1–2; Philippians 4:10– 13; Philippians 2:3–4; Proverbs 31:12; 1 Corinthians 7:34; Titus 2:3–4; Titus 2:4–5; James 1:19; Ephesians 4:32; 1 Corinthians 7:1–5; Luke 2:37; Colossians 4:2; Proverbs 31:27; 1 Timothy 5:14; 1 Timothy 5:14.

Scriptures to Pray for Your Children: Matthew 22:36–40; 2 Timothy 3:15; Psalm 97:10, 38:18; Proverbs 8:13; John 17:15, 10:10; Romans 12:9; Psalm 119:71; Hebrews 12:5–6; Daniel 1:17, 20; Proverbs 1:4; James 1:5; Romans 13:1; Ephesians 6:1–3; Hebrews 13:17; Proverbs 1:10–16; 13:20; 2 Corinthians 6:14–17; Deuteronomy 6; 1 Corinthians 6:18–20; Acts 24:16; 1 Timothy 1:19, 4:1–2; Titus 1:15–16; Psalm 23:4; Deuteronomy 10:12; Matthew 28:18– 20; Ephesians 1:3, 4:29; Ephesians 1:16–19; Philippians 1:11; Colossians 1:9; Philippians 1:9–10.

Developing Personal Prayer Habits

Rise early each day to pray with opened Bible. Daniel prayed three times daily. Pray whenever you can: as you drive, with your wife, with your children at dinner and before bedtime. You cannot pray too much!

Praying Together with Others

Pray with your spouse regularly. Make time for family prayer. Be part of your church prayer meeting or group. Christ said, "My house shall be called a house of prayer" (Matt. 21:13). The apostle Paul instructed Pastor Timothy to make prayer the first order of the church, saying prayer is key to peace in the nation (1 Tim. 2:1–8). There is nothing like a Spirit-led prayer meeting with people who love the Lord! Praying women have been standing in the prayer gap for decades. Every man must set his heart to become a praying man, lead his family in prayer, and be a strong contributor to the corporate prayer life of his church. We must be leaders in praying for our morally and spiritually troubled, divided nation—and for our national leaders. American Christians simply must respond to God's promise: "If my people who are called by my name humble themselves, and pray and seek my face and turn from their wicked ways, then I will hear from heaven and will forgive their sin and heal their land" (2 Chron. 7:14).

Prayer As Warfare

Jesus described the enemy, the devil, as a thief whose mission is to "steal, and kill and destroy" (John 10:10). Demonic forces are at war against everything good in you, your family, your church, your community, America, and every nation (Eph. 6:10–20).

The devil and his minions are out to thwart the kingdom of God and eliminate righteousness wherever he can. He hates God and hates people and will use spiritually ignorant and deceived men, women, boys, and girls to do his bidding. Men of God today, like the sons of Issachar in ancient Israel, need to understand the times and know what the church and our nation must do (1 Chron. 12:32). We must pull down Satan's strongholds, wrestle for our families, and use Spirit-led prayer and wisdom to help guide our churches and communities to prevail against the evil onslaught against us (2 Cor. 10:3–5). This is the war of the ages, and it is real.

Finally, Determine to Become a Person of Prayer

No matter how long you have been a Christian and may have neglected prayer up until now, you can become a person of prayer starting today. If you have missed the mark, it is not too late. Call upon the Lord, ask for His help, and proceed with His guidance. O Lord, make me a praying person; make me a prayer warrior! In Jesus's name, amen.

Recent polling from Barna Research shows that only about 19 percent of those who claim to be Christians actually are intentional about sharing their faith.*

Even less are successful in seeing someone make a decision to follow Christ. Maybe that is why this whole notion of sharing your faith is so intimidating for many. However, it does not have to be. The best place to start is with your story. Some call it a testimony. In a courtroom, testimony is relied on as part of the evidence in a case. As you are telling your story, you are presenting evidence for how Christ has changed your life for the better. If you are speaking with another man about your faith, think in terms of telling your story in three parts:

1. Your life before you became a follower of Christ.
2. Your encounter with Christ and your decision to follow him as your Savior and Lord.
3. Your life since becoming as a follower of Christ.

The great apostle Paul told his faith story numerous times—several of them are recorded in the Bible. You'll notice these same three parts in Acts 22.

1. Life before Christ

First of all, notice his life before Christ: Paul said,

> "I am a Jew, born in Tarsus in Cilicia, but brought up in this city, educated at the feet of Gamaliel according to the strict manner of the law of our fathers, being zealous for God as all of you are this day. I persecuted this Way to the death, binding and delivering to prison both men and women, as the high priest and the whole council of elders can bear me witness. From them I received letters to the brothers, and I journeyed toward Damascus to take those also who were there and bring them in bonds to Jerusalem to be punished." (Acts 22:3–5)

If there was ever a Jew who was steeped in religion, that Jew was Paul. His religious trophy case was filled to overflowing (v. 3). Over in Philippians 3, he pulled out and dusted off several of them. Then he described his radical commitment to his religion to the point of persecuting followers of Christ (vv. 4–5). Take time to write out what you remember about your life before your life-changing encounter with Christ. Be brief and to the point:

---

* "Sharing Faith Is Increasingly Optional to Christians," Barna, May 15, 2018, accessed November 4, 2019, https://www.barna.com/research/sharing-faith-increasingly-optional-christians/

_____

_____

_____

_____

_____

_____

2. Encounter with Christ

Paul not only told about his life before Christ, but then he shared his life-changing encounter with Christ:

> "As I was on my way and drew near to Damascus, about noon a great light from heaven suddenly shone around me. And I fell to the ground and heard a voice saying to me, 'Saul, Saul, why are you persecuting me?' And I answered, 'Who are you, Lord?' And he said to me, 'I am Jesus of Nazareth, whom you are persecuting.' Now those who were with me saw the light but did not understand the voice of the one who was speaking to me." (Acts 22:6–9)

Notice Paul said in verse 9: "Who are you, Lord?" He was told by a heavenly voice: "I am Jesus of Nazareth, whom you are persecuting." What an amazing encounter! Obviously, most people don't get blinded by a light or hear voices from heaven. However, your story of your encounter with Christ is unique, and no doubt it was (and hopefully still is) a powerful experience for you. Take time to write out your encounter with Christ and how you came to make the decision to follow him as Savior and Lord, but don't rush it. Tell what happened in detail:

_____

_____

_____

_____

_____

_____

3. Life-Change after Christ

In Acts 22:10–16, Paul began to tell about the changes in his life after his encounter with Christ:

> "And I said, 'What shall I do, Lord?' And the Lord said to me, 'Rise, and go into Damascus, and there you will be told all that is appointed for you to do.' And since I could not see because of the brightness of that light, I was led by the hand by those who were with me, and came into Damascus.
>
> "And one Ananias, a devout man according to the law, well spoken of by all the Jews who lived there, came to me, and standing by me said to me, 'Brother Saul, receive your sight.' And at that very hour I received my sight and saw him. And he said, 'The God of our fathers appointed you to know his will, to see the Righteous One and to hear a voice from his mouth; for you will be a witness for him to everyone of what you have seen and heard. And now why do you wait? Rise and be baptized and wash away your sins, calling on his name.'"

In verse 10, Paul asked, basically, "Lord, what next?" and the risen Christ told him, "You will be told all that is appointed for you to do." And then Ananias, another disciple of Jesus, communicated Paul's assignment in verses 13–16, which was basically to give his testimony and tell his story "to all people." Obviously, Paul accepted his assignment and went on to become one of the greatest leaders in the history of the Christian faith, going on missionary journeys, leading multitudes to faith in Jesus, planting churches, ordaining leaders, even giving his testimony to officials in Rome, which was the capital of the ancient world. He also experienced persecution, imprisonment, and finally death for his faith. Again, Paul's story can be intimidating, but it doesn't need to be. Just think about how your life has changed since you began following Christ. Write down some of your thoughts. Remember, you are trying to offer compelling evidence.

Having read how Paul told his faith story, use the outline above and write out yours. Once you have written it, read through it and prayerfully edit it. After you feel good about it, practice sharing it with another trusted and seasoned believer, preferably someone who has successfully helped lead someone else to faith in Christ. Then you may want to go back and edit it again as you may have thought about a better way to communicate it. Finally, pray for God to open a door of opportunity to share your faith story with someone. Pray that the Holy Spirit will prepare the way for you and do only what He can do. At the end of our best efforts to share Christ, it is still up to God and the individual.